THE WAY
PEOPLE
LIVE

Life During the Great Depression

Titles in The Way People Live series include:

THE WAY
PEOPLE
LIVE

Life During the Great Depression

by Dennis Nishi

Lucent Books, P.O. Box 289011, San Diego, CA 92198-9011

Library of Congress Cataloging-in-Publication Data

Nishi, Dennis, 1967–
    Life during the Great Depression / by Dennis Nishi.
      p.   cm. — (The way people live)
    Includes bibliographical references (p.   ) and index.
    Summary: Describes daily life of Americans during the Great
Depression, as well as some of the lasting changes that occurred such as
the increased power of the federal government and technological and
cultural innovations.
    ISBN 1-56006-381-5 (alk. paper)
    1. United States—Social life and customs—1918–1945—Juvenile
literature.   2. Depressions—1929—United States—Juvenile literature.
3. United States—Economic conditions—1918–1945—Juvenile literature.
[1. Depressions—1929.   2. United States—Social life and customs—
1918–1945.]   I. Title.   II. Series.
E169.N67   1998
973.91'6—dc21   97-33030
                                                  CIP
                                                  AC

Contents

Discovering the Humanity in Us All

The Way People Live series focuses on pockets of human culture. Some of these are current cultures, like the Eskimos of the Arctic; others no longer exist, such as the Jewish ghetto in Warsaw during World War II. What many of these cultural pockets share, however, is the fact that they have been viewed before, but not completely understood.

To really understand any culture, it is necessary to strip the mind of the common notions we hold about groups of people. These stereotypes are the archenemies of learning. It does not even matter whether the stereotypes are positive or negative; they are confining and tight. Removing them is a challenge that's not easily met, as anyone who has ever tried it will admit. Ideas that do not fit into the templates we create are unwelcome visitors—ones we would prefer remain quietly in a corner or forgotten room.

The cowboy of the Old West is a good example of such confining roles. The cowboy was courageous, yet soft-spoken. His time (it is always a he, in our template) was spent alternatively saving a rancher's daughter from certain death on a runaway stagecoach, or shooting it out with rustlers. At times, of course, he was likely to get a little crazy in town after a trail drive, but for the most part, he was the epitome of inner strength. It is disconcerting to find out that the cowboy is human, even a bit childish. Can it really be true that cowboys would line up to help the cook on the trail drive grind coffee, just hoping he would give them a little stick of pep-

permint candy that came with the coffee shipment? The idea of tough cowboys vying with one another to help "Coosie" (as they called their cooks) for a bit of candy seems silly and out of place.

So is the vision of Eskimos playing video games and watching MTV, living in prefab housing in the Arctic. It just does not fit with what "Eskimo" means. We are far more comfortable with snow igloos and whale blubber, harpoons and kayaks.

Although the cultures dealt with in Lucent's The Way People Live series are often historically and socially well known, the emphasis is on the personal aspects of life. Groups of people, while unquestionably affected by their politics and their governmental structures, are more than those institutions. How do people in a particular time and place educate their children? What do they eat? And how do they build their houses? What kinds of work do they do? What kinds of games do they enjoy? The answers to these questions bring these cultures to life. People's lives are revealed in the particulars and only by knowing the particulars can we understand these cultures' will to survive and their moments of weakness and greatness.

This is not to say that understanding politics does not help to understand a culture. There is no question that the Warsaw ghetto, for example, was a culture that was brought about by the politics and social ideas of Adolf Hitler and the Third Reich. But the Jews who were crowded together in the ghetto cannot be understood by the Reich's politics. Their life was a day-to-day battle for existence, and the creativity and methods they used to prolong their lives is a vital story of human perseverance that would be denied by focusing only on the institutions of Hitler's Germany. Knowing that children as young as five or six outwitted Nazi guards on a daily basis, that Jewish policemen helped the Germans control the ghetto, that children attended secret schools in the ghetto and even earned diplomas—these are the things that reveal the fabric of life, that can inspire, intrigue, and amaze.

Books in The Way People Live series allow both the casual reader and the student to see humans as victims, heroes, and onlookers. And although humans act in ways that can fill us with feelings of sorrow and revulsion, it is important to remember that "hero," "predator," and "victim" are dangerous terms. Heaping undue pity or praise on people reduces them to objects, and strips them of their humanity.

Seeing the Jews of Warsaw only as victims is to deny their humanity. Seeing them only as they appear in surviving photos, staring at the camera with infinite sadness, is limiting, both to them and to those who want to understand them. To an object of pity, the only appropriate response becomes "Those poor creatures!" and that reduces both the quality of their struggle and the depth of their despair. No one is served by such two-dimensional views of people and their cultures.

With this in mind, The Way People Live series strives to flesh out the traditional, two-dimensional views of people in various cultures and historical circumstances. Using a wide variety of primary quotations—the words not only of the politicians and government leaders, but of the real people whose lives are being examined—each book in the series attempts to show an honest and complete picture of a culture removed from our own by time or space.

By examining cultures in this way, the reader will notice not only the glaring differences from his or her own culture, but also will be struck by the similarities. For indeed, people share common needs—warmth, good company, stability, and affirmation from others. Ultimately, seeing how people really live, or have lived can only enrich our understanding of ourselves.

A National Blight

I'd get up at five in the morning and head for the waterfront. Outside the Spreckles sugar refinery, outside the gates there would be a thousand men. You know dang well there's only three or four jobs.

—Ed Paulsen, an unemployed worker interviewed by Studs Terkel in *Hard Times*

Mention the Great Depression, and people often think first of the poor farmers of the Oklahoma Panhandle whose livelihoods were blown into the sky by years of drought and dust storms. But their hardship is one of many in a bleak period of American history that spans the years from 1929 to 1939. The Great Depression had a devastating impact on the nation, spreading across the countryside and bringing hardship to big cities and small towns alike. No social, racial, or economic class was excluded. Farmers, bankers, bricklayers, clergymen, and auto workers were affected indiscriminately. Black, white, Latino; the formerly rich, the middle class, and the poor—all of whom had been laid off from their jobs—huddled together outside public employment offices and in bread lines that stretched for blocks.

A Job, Any Job

It was the same scene in every major city— mobs of jobless people crowded the docks and factories, vying for any work at all, hoping that it would pay enough to buy food and clothing for their families. Often the only jobs available were hazardous and low-paying ones. George W. Van Amber of Menomonie, Wisconsin, who took a job painting a suspension bridge over the Columbia River, makes this very clear: "This was scary because it was 63 feet above the water and to have fallen was sure death. I worked on a 12-inch wide plank. That's why the job was available. Not many people were willing to risk it. I worked there two days and that was enough for me."[1]

Many men who did find work often failed to make enough to support their families on the very modest wages available at the time. Wives and even children joined the workforce and often provided the only sustaining income. And while the two-income family is commonplace today, in the twenties and thirties women were openly discouraged from working.

Not everybody, however, suffered from the country's financial and employment ills. While large numbers of businesses and banks failed every day, shrewd financiers who survived the stock market crash of 1929 were buying bankrupt companies and acquiring foreclosed farms from banks at rock-bottom prices. It was also a lucrative time for bootleggers, who sold liquor they either obtained from illicit distillers operating close to home or smuggled into the country from foreign ships anchored outside national waters. The unpopular and unsuccessful Eighteenth Amendment to the Constitution, better known as

Prohibition, backfired in a way its proponents had not anticipated, giving birth to a new underground economy of organized crime. Famous crime bosses like Al "Scarface" Capone got their start during Prohibition, keeping illegal saloons called speakeasies well supplied with liquor.

Not a Decade of Idleness

Unemployment may have reached unprecedented levels during the Depression, but America was not idle. More than ever people needed to occupy themselves with something other than their troubles. The thirties gave birth to many fads that allowed anybody with a little imagination and a lot of patience to earn a few seconds of fame in the record books. Tree sitting, flagpole sitting, marathon dancing, and six-day bicycle races were a few of the challenges that tested the grit of adventuresome individuals like William "Torchy" Peden, the greatest six-day rider in the short-lived history of the sport.

The thirties also experienced a cultural and technological renaissance that ushered in a new range of media. Radio quickly became

The Great Depression affected people from all walks of life. This photo of a mother and her children living in poverty is just one of many famous images captured from the period.

Unusual record-breaking stunts were common diversions during the Depression. Here, a flagpole sitter is fed donuts while standing on his head high above New York City.

an indispensable fixture in home life, providing a rich source of news and cheap entertainment. The acceptance of sound motion pictures—popularly known as "talkies"—signaled the end of the silent film era, and television, which was in its infancy, amazed the crowds at the 1939 New York World's Fair. Box office receipts at local movie houses dipped early in the Depression but would rise to new heights, as millions of people a week laid down 25 to 35 cents a ticket to see stars like Clark Gable and Shirley Temple. Comic books, comic strips, and the chunky dime novels known as "big little books" also exploded in popularity

partly because they portrayed new kinds of heroes that transported distressed readers away from their problems to strange and exotic places.

It may be that no experience in American history will be as revealing as the Great Depression, during which so many different people were stripped not only of their dignity but of the most basic staples of living as well. Despite crushing hardships, many people adapted, survived, and even flourished. It was a decade of new experiences that would enrich every aspect of modern life. It was a decade of perseverance, ingenuity, and invention.

Uncertain Times

Although the roots had been growing undetected below the surface long before 1929, experts recognize October 29, 1929, "Black Tuesday," as the beginning of the Great Depression. Stock market prices, which had been climbing at a frantic pace for years, peaked and plummeted, sending bankers and speculators into a panic. By the end of 1929, tens of billions of dollars had been lost by investors and brokers who had indulged in the potentially risky practice of buying stocks on margin. Buying on margin allowed an investor to acquire a portion of stock on credit from a broker. The broker then borrowed the money from a bank, using the stock to be purchased on margin as collateral. If stock prices rose, the investor stood to make a big profit. If the stock lost value, the bank could demand partial or full payment immediately. Many people bought large amounts of stock for very little down, an abuse of credit that was halted by securities laws passed by Congress in the wake of the crash. Excessive buying on margin destabilized the stock market system of the 1920s and is considered one of the primary causes of the Depression.

Over a million ordinary people—doctors, shoeshine boys, file clerks, and waitresses— invested their life savings in stocks but lost their livelihoods in the speculation frenzy. Because of the loss of income and the perception of a crisis, consumption dropped and industry reacted by curbing production and laying off workers. Despite these measures, thousands of shops and factories were forced out of business. Even the largest companies in America were not immune to the widespread effects. Companies like Westinghouse and U.S. Steel proudly maintained full workforces as long as they could but eventually had to cut wages and lay off employees.

Although the bulk of the American population did not have any stake in the stock market, everyone was caught in the economic chain reaction. A million and a half people

The New York Stock Exchange on Wall Street was the site of frenzied activity when stocks plummeted on October 29, 1929. Called Black Tuesday, this day marked the beginning of the Great Depression.

were unemployed nationwide in 1929. That number grew to 4,250,000 in 1930 and to 8,020,000 in 1931. By 1932 one in every five workers—over 12 million people—were out of work. Members of minority groups made up a large part of these numbers; they suffered the worst because of discrimination and prejudice. In Detroit, Flint, and Dearborn, Michigan, whose economies depended on the well-being of corporations like General Motors and the Ford Motor Company, unemployment peaked at 50 percent a year after the production lines stopped for retooling.

Hoover's Response

At the time of the crash, the president of the United States was Herbert Clark Hoover. Born in West Branch, Iowa, in 1874, Hoover was a graduate of Stanford University in California and had been a mining engineer. He was respected worldwide for his relief efforts in Europe after World War I and for his praiseworthy service as secretary of commerce under President Warren G. Harding. Although overwhelmingly elected in 1928 on the wave of prosperity that characterized the 1920s, Hoover had the misfortune to take office on the eve of the worst economic period in American history. When the bottom fell out of the market and the unemployment figures towered, Hoover refused to give direct handouts or contribute to anything resembling the English "dole" system of unemployment relief. He wanted to keep the rugged spirit of the American people strong. Hoover wanted to nurture self-reliance and individual initiative, the pioneer traits that built America.

In one of his campaign speeches Hoover had denounced government involvement, stating: "I do not believe that the power of and duty of the general government ought to be extended to the relief of individual suffering. The lesson should be constantly enforced that though the people support the Government, the Government should not support the people." Hoover firmly believed private charities were responsible for helping the needy and even launched a campaign to promote public

Prices Plummet

Studs Terkel's oral history Hard Times *contains this description of the days after Black Tuesday. The speaker, Arthur Robinson, was a New York businessman who weathered the stock market crash.*

"October 29, 1929, yeah. A frenzy. I must have gotten calls from a dozen and a half friends who were desperate. In each case, there was no sense in loaning them the money that they would give the broker. Tomorrow they'd be worse off than yesterday. Suicides, left and right made a terrific impression on me, of course. People I knew. It was heart breaking. One day, you saw the prices at a hundred, the next day at $20, at $15. On Wall Street, the people walked around like zombies. It was like [the movie] *Death Takes a Holiday*. It was very dark. You saw people who yesterday rode around in Cadillacs lucky now to have carfare. One of my friends said to me, 'If things keep on as they are, we'll all have to go begging.' I asked, 'Who from?'"

President Hoover did not believe that people affected by the Depression should look to the U.S. government for unemployment relief or food provisions, thus forcing the masses to rely on ill-equipped city and state assistance programs.

it was estimated as many as 750,000 farms were lost through bankruptcy. In Arkansas, a group of starving farmers took matters into their own hands and seized food from the Red Cross to feed their families. Organized looting of food became a national phenomenon in the city as well as in agricultural areas. Windows were broken during the night and stores looted, and groups of hungry men bullied merchants into giving them food. City and state assistance programs were not prepared to deal with huge numbers of unemployed people, and private organizations like the Red Cross were quickly overwhelmed. In New York, relief organizations reported a 200 percent increase in aid within a year. City emergency public assistance programs were so overextended that it was estimated that only one-third of the people who needed help ever received any. Humorist Will Rogers wrote, "You let this country go hungry, and they are going to eat no matter what happens to Budgets, Income Taxes or Wall Street Values. Washington musn't forget who rules when it comes to a showdown."[3]

volunteerism. Unfortunately, Hoover underestimated the severity of the crisis. The Depression was not "a passing incident in our national lives,"[2] nor would it end in sixty days, as he assured America in his early speeches.

Starvation was being reported from cities, and unemployment was reaching critical levels. Life in rural areas, which had been plagued by drought, overproduction, and debt for years, continued to worsen as prices spiraled downward. Between 1930 and 1935

President Hoover's refusal to give federal support to struggling citizens was often satirized in political cartoons.

The Reconstruction Finance Corporation

Relying on his own philosophy, President Hoover devised an answer to the problems of the troubled economy. The crux of his solution was to use a top-down economic program that would support business and banks. After all, if a bank went out of business, it took the life savings of all its depositors with it and contributed to the disaster. And if American business were allowed to go bankrupt, who would hire the unemployed? Supporting business and stimulating trade would, in theory, create jobs, thus causing money to "trickle down" to the people on the bottom of an imaginary pyramid. A regular paycheck meant that money was available to spend on food, clothing, and other goods, which in turn increased demand for products. Increased demand would prompt businesses to increase their output of products and hire more workers to make them. Yet when Hoover proposed the plan to industry leaders, he found them to be uncooperative. They preferred to lay off workers, reduce wages, and cut working hours to salvage profit margins.

Realizing that government would have to step in, Hoover reluctantly sought enactment of a bill that would allocate $2 billion to keep ailing railroads, mines, banks, and insurance companies afloat. He established a government bank for banks called the Reconstruction Finance Corporation (RFC). Many critics disapproved of the RFC, which gave money to an alleged source of the Depression and not to the people who really needed it. When conditions seemed to worsen around the country, Hoover grudgingly agreed to allow the RFC to lend relief money to hard-pressed states. Hoover also rallied Congress to increase public works spending to create jobs building bridges, harbors, and buildings. One of the biggest construction projects undertaken in the 1930s was the building of Hoover Dam on the Colorado River.

The Bonus Expeditionary Force

In the summer of 1932, at the peak of the Depression, thousands of veterans of the First World War marched into Washington, D.C., to petition Congress to pay them immediately a wartime "bonus" scheduled to be paid in 1945. Led by Walter Waters, a former army medic with the 146th Field Artillery, the march began with a modest group of a hundred men who had been laid off from their jobs at a canning factory in Portland, Oregon.

The majority of the marchers were unemployed and desperate, but they agreed to conduct themselves in a disciplined military manner. Transportation to Washington was a catch-as-catch-can affair, but most hopped freight trains or hitchhiked. Throughout the journey eastward, the railroad companies tried unsuccessfully to deter the efforts of the determined veterans, who became known as the Bonus Army. The confrontations were tense at times but never violent. An impasse in St. Louis between the B&O Railroad Company and Waters's group brought needed publicity and support. When other down-and-out vets from across the nation learned of the march from the newspapers, many joined the expedition.

As the Bonus Army's numbers rose to twenty-five thousand over the next two months, Hoovervilles (tarpaper shantytowns named after the president) sprang up all around the open fields of Washington and in abandoned buildings. One of the biggest Hoovervilles was "Camp Marks," built near

Known as the Bonus Army, these unemployed World War I veterans marched to Washington, D.C., in 1932 seeking early payment of a wartime bonus meant to be distributed in 1945.

the heavily polluted Anacostia River, a tributary of the Potomac. In a muddy, mosquito-infested field called Anacostia Flats, fifteen thousand veterans and their families lived peacefully together in a surprisingly well-ordered community. Shelters were constructed out of flattened auto parts and planks of wood for ground cover, and dried grass served as bedding. Some resourceful men dug caves out of the banks of the river to sleep in. As the veterans settled in, they eventually built more permanent wood structures.

"That field at Anacostia looked like a cross between a Congo Village, a trash pile, a picnic ground and a tourist camp," said Waters in his book recounting his experiences as de facto Bonus Army general. Interestingly,

Waters gives credit to Washington police superintendent Chief Pelham H. Glassford, a former brigadier general in the army, for helping the veterans, but not to President Hoover. Yet Hoover, through Glassford, quietly supplied the veterans with army cots, blankets, and hot food. Whereas Glassford was openly sympathetic to the veterans' efforts, Hoover chose to help without making a public display of support. Unfortunately, this decision gave the president an undeserved appearance of callousness. Ironically, however, the president and the leader of the homeless troops shared a distaste for the philosophy of "something for nothing." In his autobiography, Waters describes what charity does to initiative:

As a result of twenty-five thousand men joining the Bonus Army's cause, makeshift shantytowns, nicknamed Hoovervilles, appeared throughout the nation's capital.

Charity does keep a body alive after a fashion, but it reduces to a minimum any satisfaction in living; it prevents actual physical suffering but at the expense of mental torture. In time, taken in regular doses it can have but one ending, the complete annihilation of a man's faith in himself and the complete rout of the desire that every decent man should have to improve himself and his position in society.[4]

Representative Edward Eslick of Tennessee spoke before his peers in support of the veterans. He had visited the camps on numerous occasions and was greeted warmly. In the middle of a debate over a bill to allow the release of some of the bonus money for immediate payment to the marchers, he died of a heart attack. The following day the bill passed the House, 211 to 176, with 40 abstaining. If ratified in the Senate, the bonus bill would have cost the country more than the tax receipts for the entire year. Hoover

sympathized with the veterans but feared the economic repercussions of the cash outlay the bill would authorize. Throughout his presidency he had tried to curb a growing national debt. He was outspokenly against the measure and helped defeat the bill in the Senate, 62 to 18. Many of the veterans with families bitterly abandoned the camps, and indeed Hoover encouraged passage of a transportation loan bill that set aside $100,000 to help the marchers to return to their homes. Still, many discouraged families remained in Washington hoping the situation would improve.

Fearing the potential health problems and wary after an incident involving a shooting between a policeman and a group of unarmed veterans, Hoover ordered U.S. troops commanded by army chief of staff Douglas MacArthur, his young adjutant, Dwight D. Eisenhower (a future president of the United States), and Major George S. Patton to "escort" anyone who remained out of the city. An overzealous MacArthur deliberately exceeded the limits of Hoover's executive order, crossed the bridge into a Bonus Army encampment, and burned the shantytown, routing the remaining campers with water hoses, bayonets, and tear gas. The public was outraged, and the press was highly critical. Hoover's reelection aspirations, weakened by the continuing Depression, were further damaged by the Bonus Army incident.

The Beginning of the End

The end of Hoover's term was met with hostility from all sides. Congress was uncooperative, and an unsympathetic press continued to rebuke him. Most of Hoover's attempts to rid the nation of the Depression had fallen short, serving only to earn him a reputation for be-

Army chief of staff Douglas MacArthur (left) led the effort to forcibly remove the Bonus Army veterans from their shantytowns in Washington, D.C.

ing insensitive and uncaring. His name undeservedly became synonymous with the blight and worked its way into the language in various negative expressions: Hoover flags were empty pockets turned inside out, Hoover hogs were the jackrabbits farmers caught for food, and Hoovervilles were squalid villages of homeless people. The Democrats took full advantage of these perceptions in their campaign and were even accused by Hooverites of allowing the Depression to worsen for their own benefit. Although the Republicans nominated Hoover to run for a second term in 1932, a despondent president continued to battle the Depression alone, without the support of either side in Congress.

New President, New Deal

Americans expressed their dissatisfaction with the Hoover administration at the polls in November 1932. All but six states overwhelmingly elected Democratic nominee Franklin Delano Roosevelt the thirty-second president of the United States. Unlike Hoover, who was trained as an engineer, Roosevelt was a charismatic politician who knew how to use the press and was adept at rallying people to his cause. These talents would help him achieve an unprecedented series of four victorious runs for the office of president. Roosevelt had been crippled by polio as an adult but refused to let the disability hinder his political career. With the invaluable help of his wife, Eleanor (who was also his cousin), and an unspoken agreement with the press, most of the country was not aware of his paralysis. It was agreed that nothing should be allowed to diminish the president's image in those desperate times. The country needed to be guided by a strong leader who was perceived as being whole in body as well as in mind and spirit.

Upon election, Roosevelt moved quickly to attack the Depression head on. One of his campaign promises, to maintain a balanced budget, proved to be an impossible task. Roosevelt had been watching conditions worsen from the sidelines throughout the last days of Hoover's term. To help devise solutions to the economic problems, the new president consulted with his "brain trust," a group of advisers who helped him draft emergency legislation. The brain trust differed from the business and political advisers of past chief executives because it was composed of liberal university scholars and theorists. Roosevelt and his brain trust sought to enact radical new reforms that would greatly expand the role of

government and hopefully return prosperity to the country. In a 1932 campaign speech Roosevelt had proclaimed, "The country needs and, unless I mistake its temper, demands bold, persistent experimentation. It is common sense to take a method and try it. If it fails, admit it frankly and try another. But above all, try something."[5]

The First Hundred Days

In March 1933 Roosevelt gave his first inaugural address over the radio to a beleaguered nation—the first president in history to speak directly to the public, rather than solely to the dignitaries attending the ceremony. He promised immediate action, emphasizing that the country must be built from the bottom up as opposed to the top-down approach of the Hoover administration. Desperate for action and public approval, Congress granted Roosevelt broad "blank check" powers, virtually rubber-stamping measures proposed and drafted in the executive office without the usual lengthy debates. Almost every measure he proposed over the next hundred days was approved, heralding an unprecedented flood of new bills designed to relieve poverty, reduce unemployment, and speed economic recovery.

Ironically, Roosevelt's first priority as president was to save the banks, the same strategy Hoover had proposed. During the final four months of Hoover's term, the American banking system teetered on the verge of collapse. Hoover had begged the president-elect to lend his support to some interim measures Hoover believed might halt the slide. But Roosevelt refused to become involved in anything connected with Hoover, fearing it would taint his efforts when he took office.

Roosevelt had his own thoughts on how to save the country's ailing banks, and one of

Democratic nominee Franklin Delano Roosevelt succeeded Hoover as president in 1933.

Raymond Moley was one of the original members of Roosevelt's brain trust. A former professor of government and public law at Columbia University, Moley had advised Roosevelt when the future president was governor of New York. Interviewed by Studs Terkel for the book Hard Times, *Moley recalls how his disapproval of Roosevelt's increasingly radical relief policies led to his resignation.*

"Unemployment insurance is a welfare measure. It isn't insurance in any sense of the word. More and more people were living off fewer and fewer people. That's when the unsound practices began. . . . In 1935, I took a firm stand. I said welfare is a narcotic, because it will never end. We'll have to stop this business and put people to work. The best way to put people to work is to encourage the development of industrial science. The Government can't put people to work. I began to have my doubts in 1935. I had many arguments with him [Roosevelt]. . . . Finally, in '36, in the middle of the year, I quit. I never went back to him again."

---

his first acts as president was to declare a four-day bank holiday to give panicky citizens time to calm down and Congress time to come up with remedial legislation. In eight hours the Emergency Banking Relief Act of 1933, which was designed to stabilize the system by providing loans through the RFC, was drafted and put before both houses of Congress. The bill passed through the system so quickly that the ink was still wet on the documents when they arrived at the Capitol. Three months later the more important Glass-Steagall Act was enacted, separating comercial banking from investment banking and creating the Federal Deposit Insurance Corporation (FDIC). The FDIC insured the savings of depositors up to $5,000 (in contrast, the FDIC insures amounts up to $100,000 today) and proved to be one of the New Deal's most important programs. No longer would depositors have to fear losing their life savings when banks got into trouble. The government would now insure people's deposits, providing a sense of security when times were bad.

With the end of the banking crisis, America's confidence began to return. People stopped hoarding money, and the prices of goods and securities rose slightly. At Roosevelt's request, Congress legalized the sale of a weak form of beer in 1933, reviving the liquor industry and effectively ending Prohibition.

The Civilian Conservation Corps

Overwhelming unemployment was one of the most urgent issues Roosevelt committed himself to addressing. By the time he stepped into office, the nation's unemployment numbers were staggering. The Civilian Conservation Corps (CCC) was Roosevelt's own brainchild, designed to address both unemployment and the need to preserve the country's natural resources. It became one of the New Deal's most high profile and successful programs during the Depression. Created through the Unemployment Relief Act and placed under the jurisdiction of the Department of Labor, the CCC took 3 million single

Roosevelt was the first president whose inaugural address was broadcast over public radio. In this famous address, FDR announced plans for his New Deal.

men between the ages of seventeen and twenty-three off city streets and put them into the forests. They were paid $30 a month (two-thirds of which was sent home) to plant trees, dig ditches, build reservoirs, and fight fires. All the CCC members were volunteers, and their families were on relief. They lived in the national forests in open air camps operated by army reserve officers. The "three C's," as it was called, was one of the most expensive New Deal programs, but it also proved to be one of the most effective. The following report was recorded by interviewer Jane Leary, who also owed her job to a government program, the Works Progress Administration (WPA):

I got one son nineteen [notes Leary's interviewee, a mother of eleven]. He's just come home from the CCCs and what a difference in a boy. When he went he had the idea that everybody wuz pickin' on him an' I was scared he'd get in with the wrong crowd. He'd wanta go to a show an' I wun't have the money fur him or ta buy him a pack a cigarettes an' ya know how it is. Now he's home an' how he changed. Don't go round lookin' fur a crowd ta rob somebody's pear tree or something. And I cun't go round followin' after 'leven. So I wuz glad fur the CCC. An' now I got another boy. He's seventeen and he kin go in September. But he's no trouble ta me. I'm aspeakin' the truth when I say that boy ain't been no trouble ta me since he wuz born. But his brother now; he's sixteen. If he wuz seventeen I'd shoe him off ta the camp tomorrow an' see if that would make a man a him.[6]

The NRA and the WPA

The National Industrial Recovery Act (NIRA) and its offspring the National Recovery Ad-

In an effort to create jobs and preserve natural resources, Roosevelt created the Civilian Conservation Corps. This program paid young men to perform such jobs as building reservoirs, planting trees, and fighting fires.

The National Recovery Administration sought to assist industry and labor by regulating work standards.

ministration (NRA) were the most inspired New Deal plans. Represented by a big blue eagle, the NRA was designed to provide long-term solutions. The NRA sought to assist both industry and labor with 550 voluntary codes and standards. The codes set minimum wages, lowered working hours, and banned child labor and price fixing. The plan yielded some gains in production and employment, but there were conflicts as well. Under the NRA production costs and the cost of living rose, leaving the buying power of wages behind. The NRA also hurt small businesses, allowing big companies to squeeze out struggling competitors, exploit labor, and price-gouge the public. On May 27, 1935, the Supreme Court unanimously declared the parent act, the NIRA, unconstitutional. The high-flying NRA eagle fell flat, but some of its legacies, such as shorter working hours and the five-day work-week, remain today.

A program to hire workers for public works projects like Hoover Dam had begun during the Hoover administration. Roosevelt took the program in 1935 and gave it a needed push, turning it into the Works Progress Administration. Over the life of the program, the WPA gave jobs instead of handouts to 8.5 million people to build roads, bridges, and parks. The WPA also found part-time jobs for students and employed thousands of artists and writers through the Arts Projects section. The WPA hired 16,000 people in music, 6,500 in literature, 12,500 in the theater, and 5,000 in other arts, giving 150 million Americans a chance to enjoy the arts through concerts and theater productions. Some participants in the Federal Writers' Project who went on to gain national recognition were novelists John Steinbeck, Ralph Ellison, Margaret Walker, Saul Bellow, John Cheever, Zora Neale Hurston, and Richard Wright. Actors and playwrights like Orson Welles and John Houseman were employed by the Federal Theater Project.

Other Alphabet Agencies

The Tennessee Valley Authority (TVA) exceeded Roosevelt's expectations by revitalizing an entire region. The TVA was authorized to manage local resources and develop the

A Growing Concern

This letter from Down & Out in the Great Depression: Letters from the "Forgotten Man," *edited by Robert McElvaine, expresses the growing concern of many Americans over the New Deal's seemingly socialistic and antibusiness approach to relief. The writer, a man from Hornell, New York, addresses one of his representatives in Washington.*

"My Dear Senator:

It seems very apparent to me that the Administration at Washington is accelerating its pace towards socialism and communism. Nearly every public statement from Washington is against the stimulation of business which would in the end create employment. Everyone is sympathetic to the cause of creating more jobs and better wages for labor; but, a program continually promoting labor troubles, higher wages, shorter hours, and less profits for business, would seem to me to be leading us fast to a condition where the Government must more and more expand its relief activities, and will lead in the end to disaster to all classes. I believe that every citizen is entitled to know the policy of all Government, and I am so confused that I wish you would write me and advise me whether it is the policy of this Administration, of which you are a very important part, to further discourage business enterprise, and eventually set up a program which eliminates private industry and effort, and replaces it with Government control of industry and labor—call it what you will: socialism, fascism, or communism, or by any other name. I am not addicted to annoying public office holders with correspondence, but if there are any private rights left in this country, then I would appreciate an early reply to this letter, so that I may take such action as is still possible, to protect myself and family.

With kindest personal regards,

Yours truly,
W. L. C."

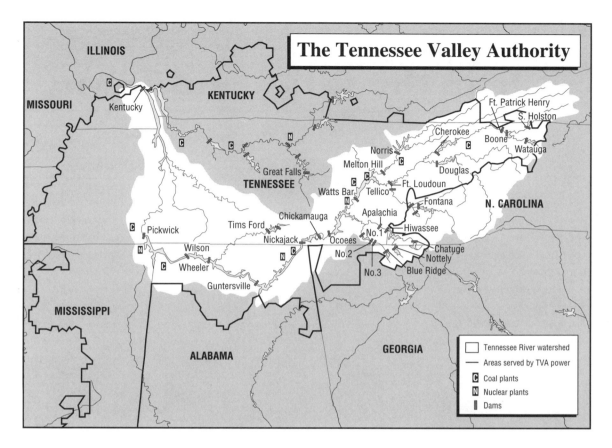

Tennessee Valley by constructing a series of hydroelectric dams that would provide cheap power. It was the first case of direct federal involvement in the industry. Roosevelt described the TVA as a corporation empowered by the government but having the flexibility and drive of private enterprise.

The Federal Emergency Relief Administration (FERA) was created in 1933 and granted $3 billion to states to fund work projects relief for unemployed adults. The Agricultural Adjustment Act (AAA) helped preserve farming interests with crop reduction subsidies to stabilize prices and loans for overdue mortgages. The Home Owners' Loan Corporation (HOLC) helped save homes from foreclosure by allowing people to refinance their property with low-interest loans.

Putting Ideas and People to Work

The New Deal was a time of experimentation and putting new ideas and theories to work. Although Roosevelt's full frontal assault did not cure the Depression, it did ease hard times on all levels by addressing basic needs and giving hope to Americans. Ironically it would take an even bigger crisis, the Second World War, to fully revive the American economy. Roosevelt succinctly pointed out in his second inaugural address, "I see one-third of a nation ill-housed, ill-clad, ill-nourished . . . the test of our progress is not whether we add more to the abundance of those who have much; it is whether we provide enough for those who have too little."[7]

Life in the Cities and Towns

American cities experienced fabulous growth during the 1920s. They became gleaming symbols of progress and technology. New manufacturing processes created a boom in production, consumption, and employment. The success of the automobile and the paving of new roads and highways linked small towns to big cities. Thousands of people were lured out of the country with the promise of high-paying jobs. Cities proudly grew upward as well as outward in a battle for the tallest buildings. In 1931 the Empire State Building in New York City clinched that honor at 1,250 feet. It was an engineering marvel tall enough to be struck by a B-25 bomber caught in a fog bank years later.

The Empire State Building (left) symbolized the booming economic growth of the 1920s.

A breadline near the Brooklyn Bridge in New York. With seventeen thousand families evicted from their homes each month during the peak of the Depression, public assistance programs were quickly overwhelmed.

Unfortunately, civic improvement could not deter the oncoming crisis. After the 1929 crash, businesses were failing at an appalling rate and the gleaming buildings and factories of more prosperous times were closed, boarded up, and taken over by a wave of homeless people who needed shelter. There were no sellers or buyers in the market, and new building projects were stopped so that funds could be diverted to relief. Between 1929 and 1932 residential construction declined by 82 percent in urban regions and by 75 percent in other areas. Construction income fell from $6.6 billion in 1929 to $1.3 billion in 1932.

Coming In from the Cold

As the Depression deepened, cities attracted beaten people from all parts of the country. Farmers whose livelihoods had been foreclosed packed up their families and moved into the cities. Hoboes and other itinerants sought shelter in cities during harsh winters. City dwellers themselves were not immune to the ails of the nation. Thousands of unemployed residents who could not pay their rent or mortgages were evicted into the world of public assistance and bread lines. At the peak of the Depression, seventeen thousand families were put out on the street each month. Although residents were given priority over newcomers for local aid, there were too many other residents standing in the same lines waiting for a check or a bowl of soup. Municipal resources were overwhelmed quickly, and city agencies resorted to thinning relief payments to below the cost of living and watering down the soup to help more people over a longer time.

Many cities just ran out of money and were even forced to pay city employees in scrip (a temporary voucher, redeemable for food and other products). At the height of the Depression Chicago had half a million unemployed, and in New York the jobless figure topped a million. With so many taxpayers both jobless and homeless, American cities lost a major source of income. Relief budgets meant to last a year were spent in several months.

At President Hoover's beckoning, charities had stepped in to help ease the burden on municipal resources. Hoover was a firm believer in volunteerism. Feeling that each

In 1930 some six thousand unemployed workers sold apples in New York City. Their presence began a trend in street vending.

houses and give the unemployed a way to make a little money, they sold apples on credit. The ploy worked. Months later a shivering apple vendor could be found standing over a fruit crate on the corner of every major American city. By the end of November there were six thousand people selling apples in New York alone. The trend spread, and suddenly there were pitchmen of all persuasions standing alongside the apple sellers, hawking everything from patent medicines to gaudy neckties. There were even chalk artists who drew figures of women on the sidewalks for passersby to appreciate with a few coins. Many cities soon passed ordinances, however, which banned the street vendors as a nuisance to the public.

The Last Resort

With no work available and relief checks that did not go far enough, there was always the corner pawnshop to turn to. Pawnshops, which lend money in exchange for the security of personal goods, have existed for thousands of years and have serviced a need for discretion in the community. During the Depression, many found that hocking a ring and a pocket watch for a few dollars could keep the car from being repossessed or pay for groceries.

The Provident Loan Society of New York was a different kind of pawnshop and one of the largest lending institutions in the country during the Depression. The Provident had twenty-two offices and lent $40 million annually, which is more money than all the pawnshop loans in New York combined. The Provident was established by New York's Private Charities Administration, patterned after state-run pawnshops in Europe. It was managed by a board of volunteers, all of whom

community was responsible for aiding people in distress, Hoover created programs that bolstered morale and encouraged charity. But the charities were themselves in trouble because they depended on contributions from a public who could not give any more. In many cities philanthropic groups of businessmen mounted relief drives, but the funds collected dwindled quickly as conditions worsened.

In 1930 the International Apple Shippers Association was faced with an oversupply of fruit and came up with a unique solution to a national problem: to clear out their ware-

where well-respected business leaders. The Provident was a nonprofit organization and lent money at an extremely unprofitable rate. The administrative costs to maintain most of the small loans exceeded the money brought in when the personal items were redeemed and interest paid. It was the interest earned on larger loans that made up for the deficit and put the organization into the black. If a borrower's property was not claimed, it was auctioned off. The Provident earned its benevolent reputation by keeping only enough money from each sale to cover the loan and interest. Any surplus was returned to the original customer. During the Depression the price for goods dropped precipitously, and fewer people returned to claim their property. The Provident adopted a more cautious lending policy but still made a profit at the end of each year.

The privately owned pawnshop had a seedy reputation for dealing in stolen goods and charging borrowers very high interest rates. This unsavory image was perpetuated by the small, run-down stores from which most pawnshops operated. But the Provident looked and operated more like a bank. The board members wanted to eliminate the stigma associated with dealing with a pawnshop. The offices of the Provident were set in a largely open space and adorned in brass and marble to look like a bank branch. The tellers were mostly men, who were all required to dress in a company-supplied outfit consisting of trousers, collared shirt, tie, and black jacket. By company policy, all clients, from the hobo to the fallen banker, were treated alike.

When There Was No Place Else to Go

With foreclosures and evictions becoming all too common, Hoovervilles rose up in every city under bridges, in abandoned lots, in city dumps, and alongside major highways across America. These makeshift shantytowns, filled with hunger, crime, and disease, provided a final refuge for people with no place left to go. Brooklyn's "Hoover City" housed six hundred residents. Another such community, in Oklahoma next to city stockyards, was home to over two thousand. The smell was overwhelming, but the cows provided milk for starving residents, who crept into the pens at night.

Hoovervilles had no electricity or running water but were usually built near rivers or fireplugs. They were not supported by the city or government in any way, so moving into such an encampment required no registration or security deposit. Prospective residents simply looked around and picked a spot. City

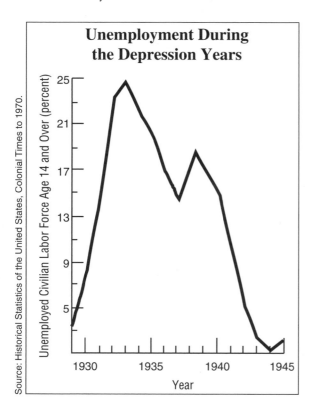

Unemployment During the Depression Years

Source: Historical Statistics of the United States, Colonial Times to 1970.

Unemployed Civilian Labor Force Age 14 and Over (percent)

25
21
17
13
9
5

1930   1935   1940   1945
Year

dumps, construction sites, and trash bins provided materials for constructing shelters. The gutted husks of old cars made acceptable homes, as did stacks of fruit boxes and worn tires. If a shelter was built well enough, a resident could sell it. There was always turnover, since people continually came and went. A good prebuilt home could easily be worth as much as $50.

Despite zoning violations and health hazards, many Hoovervilles were allowed to exist. Some cities even lent tracts of public land for the cultivation of small gardens. Not everybody was tolerant, however. Many Hoovervilles were raided and burned down by sheriffs and vigilante groups. Former hobo Ed Paulsen recalls his experiences with members of various American Legion posts:

> They were the most vicious enemies of this drifting, reckless, hungry crowd of people. Every place I went, Hoovervilles—they were raided. This bunch of Legionnaires with those damn caps on.

Guys with baseball bats, driving them out of the jungles around the railroad grounds. Even in the little towns I lived in. I had a war with those guys by the time I was in high school. They were always the bane of my existence.[8]

The Working Class

City residents who managed to keep their jobs and houses took pay cuts or large reductions in their work schedules. A survey of fifteen hundred companies suggested that workers lost 32 percent of their pay between 1929 and 1932. Of those people, it is estimated half worked part-time. It became a financial necessity for working-class householders to take on borders and roommates. Newly arrived migrants, workers, and poor single parents who could not afford their own accommodations lived cheaply with a score of roommates and offered a small additional income for the hosts.

Unemployed "squatters" gather for a meal in a Chicago Hooverville in 1932. These men lived without electricity and running water, and they coped daily with hunger, crime, and disease.

Crowded living conditions were not uncommon in the working-class home. Extended families were formed who shared the same space, food costs, rent, and even bedding: the "hotbed" was a living arrangement in which night workers slept during the day and day workers used the same beds at night. Furnishings in working-class apartments were sparse. There were a few chairs, tables, and boxes that served as dressers. There was rarely any carpeting, and not all homes had hot water. In older buildings heat was provided through coal grates, which forced tenants to scour the neighborhood for coal or other fuel. Many people planted subsistence gardens in vacant lots or rooftops to feed themselves when grocery money was really scarce. Twenty thousand of these gardens were reported in Gary, Indiana, alone.

Interestingly enough, during the Depression people held onto their cars as long as they could financially afford them, and many held onto them even when they could not afford the expense. Will Rogers was quoted as saying: "The American people will be the first in history to ride to the poorhouse in their own automobiles."[9] The automobile was changing the landscape by forcing cities to accommodate the increasing number of cars on the road. Signs, lights, boulevards, parkway and highway construction, and even parking meters cost billions of dollars annually. Thanks to the automobile, the middle class moved out of the city into the suburbs, a region that was made more accessible by the newly constructed roads. Many moved into tract housing, which utilized mass production techniques to bring construction prices down. Large-scale housing developments were built between the 1920s and 1930s. The cheaper land also encouraged commercial development of stores and other outlets that made life more convenient and less dependent on the cities.

Many low-income apartment buildings were built before 1937 by the Public Works Administration. Under Roosevelt's New Deal program, monthly rent for these apartments averaged less than thirty dollars.

Homes

Before the Depression, suburbanites' biggest hardship was the traffic that clogged roads in and out of the city. After the crash, homeowners who had mortgage payments due every month worried about losing their homes. In March 1933, homes were being foreclosed across the nation at a rate of a thousand per day. Roosevelt created the Home Owners Loan Corporation and Farm Mortgage Act of 1933 to stem the growing number of foreclosures in both urban and rural areas. The HOLC lent money to over a million homeowners and allowed them to pay over 20 years, as opposed to the customary 5 or 10 (in contrast, a typical mortgage today

Down & Out in the Great Depression: Letters from the "Forgotten Man," *edited by Robert McElvaine, is a revealing collection of communications from ordinary people in distress to senators, congressmen, and the Roosevelts. These letters, from a wide variety of people, show Depression-era Americans to be proud, hardworking people who accepted relief only as a last resort. Many only wanted to "borrow" money and pay the loan back when they were able. Others expressed a preference for a job over relief payments. This excerpt is from a letter to the president's wife, written by an expectant mother of two in New York.*

"Dear Mrs. Roosevelt,

About a month ago I wrote you asking if you would buy some baby clothes for me with the understanding that I was to repay you as soon as my husband got enough work. Several weeks later I received a reply to apply to a Welfare Association so I might receive the aid I needed. Do you remember? Please Mrs. Roosevelt, I do not want charity, only a chance from someone who will trust me until we can get enough money to repay the amount spent for things I need. As a proof that I really am sincere, I am sending you two of my dearest possessions to keep as security, a ring my husband gave me before we were married, and a ring my mother used to wear. Perhaps the actual value of them is not high, but they are worth a lot to me. If you will consider buying the baby clothes, please keep them (rings) until I send you the money you spent. It is very hard to face bearing a baby we cannot afford to have, and the fact it is due to arrive soon, and still there is no money for the hospital or clothing, does not make it any easier. . . .

If you will get these for me I would rather no one knew about it. I promise to repay the cost of the layette as soon as possible. We will all be very grateful to you, and I will be more than happy.

Sincerely yours,

Mrs. H. E. C."

---

can run 25 to 30 years). Three billion dollars in loans was distributed throughout the life of the program. Hundreds of thousands of families were saved from foreclosure.

Another New Deal program, the Public Works Administration (PWA), sought to create decent, low-cost housing. Before the program ended in 1937, there were nearly twenty-two thousand new units, with rent averaging $26 a month. Contracting to private sources, the PWA leveled slums in the worst areas of the cities and built apartment buildings with modern conveniences like hot and cold running water and a bathroom for each dwelling unit. Tenants whose family income exceeded the requirements of the program were asked to leave. The families who could not be saved by the New Deal ended up moving back into the city and collecting relief.

The Family

The working-class family underwent tremendous strain during hard times. Traditional roles of the father as the provider and the mother as the homemaker became blurred as the entire family was forced to seek work to keep food on the table. The effect of a father's unemployment on the entire family was evident: "Bewilderment, hesitation, apathy, loss of self-confidence were the commonest marks of protracted unemployment. A man no longer cared how he looked. Unkempt hair and swarthy stubble, shoulders a-droop, a slow dragging walk."[10] In many instances the idle man just got in the way, hanging around home because there was no place else to go. Tempers grew short and tension between husband and wife resulted in quarreling. The family would lose touch with friends, especially those who were still working. Evenings were especially difficult. When the entire family was home, nothing could be hidden. Children could sense the tension between parents. Desperation crept into every part of life. Restless fathers who had had no luck finding work during the day lay awake at night worrying about how to feed the family.

As days turned into weeks, and weeks into months, the husband's clothing became frayed. Much of the household budget went to buying clothes for him, since he had to make a good impression when looking for a job or working. In cases of extreme financial difficulty, father and son shared the same clothes. Because the wife stayed home to take care of the household, her clothing needs were considered less important. She made do with what she had or could make herself. Even soap was considered an unaffordable luxury when more food could be purchased instead.

When there was no job for the father, the mother and children sought any work they could find. What few jobs were available for women and children paid very little. Children were forced to grow up faster and take on more responsibility earlier to help the entire family. The eldest sons held part-time jobs after school or worked instead of going to school. The eldest daughters took care of the

Family life during the Depression was often stressful. All family members who were old enough to work were forced to find jobs to help support the household.

Life in the Cities and Towns

younger brothers and sisters when the parents were working or looking for work. During the most difficult times, when there was no employment for anybody and the family was forced to accept relief, morale plummeted.

The women who did find work faced many obstacles. The prejudice typical of the times became worse during the Depression, as women were perceived as taking jobs normally held by men. But most of the jobs women held were considered "women's jobs" and were not always interchangeable. Women during the 1930s typically held positions in domestic service (as maids), in social work, in clerical jobs, and in primary education. Married working women were especially frowned upon, since supposedly their husbands were supporting them. But one income was not

enough in most cases. Even so, the government seemed to sanction discrimination against women: female WPA workers received only $3 a day, whereas men were paid $5, and this discrepancy in pay was imposed by NRA codes.

Harlem Rent Parties

Urban black families were also the victims of prejudice and discrimination. Many landlords would not even rent to African Americans, so tens of thousands of people lived packed together in aging tenement buildings in segregated parts of the city. To save money, two or even three families might occupy a single-family dwelling. Many of the buildings had

Many wives took in laundry and ironing to help provide for their households while their husbands looked for work.

attics, cellars, and basements converted into sparse apartment units. Some had no windows, no private baths, and perhaps not even a public bath. Those who were fortunate enough to find a bathtub installed it in the only room with running water: the kitchen. Landlords knew how difficult it was for blacks to find housing in other parts of the city and raised rents systematically, making it difficult for even the thriftiest families to hold onto money. Many landlords failed to maintain the ramshackle buildings, some of which were on the verge of being condemned, creating a health and safety hazard for tenants and neighborhood alike.

Harlem residents resorted to throwing parties to raise money to pay for housing. These "rent parties" became popular social events that featured live music, home-cooked food, and alcohol. Rent parties were advertised discreetly on little cards handed from person to person:

> Shake it and break it. Hang it on the wall.
> Sling it out the window and catch it
> before it falls.
> At a social whist [card] party given
> by _____ at _____ .
> Saturday evening, March 16, 1929.
> Music by Texas Slim. Refreshments.[11]

In the following selection from a WPA oral history recording, "Slick" Reynolds, a blackjack dealer in Harlem, recalls some of the hazards of inviting drunken strangers into the house:

> There was plenty of dough in the party racket and it used to be the mainstay of a lot of the boys who needed to make a little extra dough. But the only trouble with staging rent parties as an out-an-out hustle was the crazy crowd you had to cater to. You put out your cards, hire a piano-player, open your door an' just wait for all sorts of studs and chicks to wander in. If you were lucky, you might get through the night without any major accidents— but I never seemed to have that kinda luck. Some punch drunk broad was always breaking up my shindigs. First they'd get loaded to the gills with King Kong [an alcoholic drink], start getting rambuncktuous an' wanting to pick a fight at the drop of a hat. Some guy'd get accidentally shoved or just naturally get evil cause his ol' lady would dance more than once. . . . An' then to top it off, when the cops would come, they'd stalk through the house straight back to the kitchen and throw down half a dozen or more slugs of my likker and stuff their coat pockets with fried chicken.[12]

Discrimination Everywhere You Go

Urban black Americans were also discriminated against in the workplace. Despite being forced to work longer hours than their white counterparts, they earned considerably less money and had less job security. They were often the last hired and the first fired for what few jobs were available. And jobs that had typically been held by unskilled black workers in the city were now being taken by white workers suddenly willing to become porters, garbagemen, and domestics. Because of widespread discrimination, large numbers of black workers collected relief. In Philadelphia blacks comprised 39 percent of those on relief. Other cities had similar numbers, which gave the false impression that black workers were lazy and unreliable. Comparing modern views with those that prevailed during the

Depression, sociologist Horace Cayton notes, "To be without money is a disgrace in America today. The middle class looks upon welfare Negroes as morally corrupt because they haven't worked. But in the Depression, there were so many whites who were on relief. So the Negro would look, and he wouldn't see any great difference."[13]

Displaced southern blacks, many of whom had been tenant farmers, migrated north in record numbers. They found prejudice in the cities to be less obvious but just as pervasive as it was back home. Many southern cities and towns still had segregated public transportation, hospitals, restaurants, churches, and theaters. Although these prejudices compounded the problems blacks faced in the workplace, the working conditions in many industries were generally exploitive for both blacks and whites.

Fighting for Fair Wages

Low wages, long hours, and poor working conditions plagued many workers during the Depression. Because there was a large unemployed labor force, employers could respond to workers' complaints by threatening to replace the discontented with any of the countless idle people waiting for a job. To redress this problem, some logically looked to unions to strengthen their ability to bargain with employers. But unions also suffered during the hard times. The widespread unemployment kept union membership low during the early 1930s. Union membership had fallen to an unprecedented 2 million, down from 5 million a decade earlier. A once powerful union, the United Mine Workers, had lost much of its power as a result of the national crisis and internal conflicts. The middle and later 1930s, however, saw the largest ever increase in union membership. Thanks to the New Deal, labor unions grew to become a considerable force with political influence. The following endorsement is from a factory worker who saw an immediate improvement after his workplace was unionized:

> All the people know what a union means and what good the union does for them and even though they aint active in the union, they support it. Yeh, they're are some Communists around but no known ones you could say right out is a Communist. It's a tough trade, low paid and hell on the nerves. Since the union came in, a lot of the speed up has been reduced. That's the worst part, the speed up.[14]

The 1930s will forever hold the distinction of being a milestone decade for the organized labor movement.

After years of poor working conditions and starvation wages, the labor movement exploded into the agricultural and industrial workplace. Bloody confrontations between dissatisfied employees and company police never failed to make the headlines. This revolution for the blue-collar worker, however, was made more difficult by an economy in which jobs were scarce and profits low. Business leaders had little tolerance for unions and hired strikebreaking specialists who made millions by applying muscle, machine guns, and tear gas on cue. Constant fear of a communist uprising, aggravated by random bombing incidents, heightened tensions. There was a nationwide crusade against anybody whose patriotism was suspect, and many business owners used the "Red scare" to their advantage to disrupt union activity. The bombings and other unexplained crimes, meanwhile, prompted the passage of strict bans on criminal cooperatives.

The Red Influence

The Communist Party in America was born after the Russian Revolution of 1917. It saw a sharp drop in membership early in the 1930s. Max Shachtman, a former Communist leader, recalls the state of the party before the crash:

> Until the Crash occurred, it was thought there was something unique about American capitalism. Even the radicals felt it. They were in bad shape. The communists were wracked by internal strife. The Socialists were stagnating. Ford was paying his workers $5 a day—unprecedentedly high wages. It seemed the class struggle was coming to an end, and radicalism might disappear. But the 1929 crisis created a revolution in thought: it affected liberals and, in many cases, conservatives, as well as radicals.[15]

But with the onset of the Depression, the party grew. Communism and its philosophy ("from each according to his ability, to each according to his needs"; "the workers should own the means of production") appeared to be an ideal system to people suffering from unemployment, hunger, and discrimination. Taking power out of the hands of the few and returning it to the many seemed attractive to those who had been struck down by the system. Many people saw business and capitalism in general as the source of the Depression in the first place.

The Communist Party had many lofty goals in the 1930s, but achieved very few. The Communists were never able to destabilize the capitalist system or get anybody elected to political office. In those days, however, they aggressively asserted their politics wherever they could find an audience. They attached themselves to any conflict they noticed, including

There Is Fear in the Air

Here is another letter to Eleanor Roosevelt, excerpted from Down & Out in the Great Depression. *The writer is a man in Tennessee who worries about the possibility of a bloody workers' revolution.*

"Mrs. Franklin D. Roosevelt,
Dear Lady

Will you please warn the people of what's going to happen in America if these property owners dont quit making industrial slaves out of their laborers and working them on starvation wages, paying them a wage whereby they cannot obtain the desires of life, or else installing machinery and laying the common laborer off of his job to starve to death. We dont want a revolution in this country where innocent men, women, and children will be shot down without mercy like they are doing in Spain and also like they did in Russia. . . . Mrs. Roosevelt can we believe for a minute that our young men and young women that are growing up, being educated, educated from an eighth grade to a college education, educating them selves especially on the economical conditions of the world, are going to be willing to become industrial slaves on starvation wages? This alone will bring on a revolution if not remedied.

Yours,
Sincerely,

D. B. P."

What Proud People Must Endure

Waiting hours to collect a relief check could be a dispiriting experience to anyone. The hopelessness of long-term unemployment was an unfamiliar feeling, which intensified feelings of anger and frustration. Relief offices were a test of patience for caseworkers and recipients alike. Agency staffers were overworked and subjected to tremendous stress. Fraud was common, so applicants were forced to prove their need. In Studs Terkel's Hard Times, *caseworker Eileen Barth relates a visit to a laid-off railroad worker.*

"I was told by my supervisor that I really had to see the poverty. If the family needed clothing, I was to investigate how much clothing they had at hand. So I looked into this man's closet—(pauses, it becomes difficult)—he was a tall, gray-haired man, though not terribly old. He let me look in the closet—he was so insulted. (She weeps angrily.) He said, 'Why are you doing this?' I remember his feeling of humiliation . . . this terrible humiliation. (She can't continue. After a pause, she resumes.) He said, 'I really haven't anything to hide, but if you really must look into it . . .' I could see he was very proud. He was so deeply humiliated. And I was, too."

automotive labor strikes in Michigan, agricultural strikes in California, and the Bonus Army's march. Although the Communist Party did not invent the labor union, it did focus attention on exploited workers and contributed to the growth of organized labor.

Working in an Auto Plant

Automation revolutionized automotive production. The car assembly line became a national symbol of economic prosperity and technological advancement. Not only did it reduce the costs of production, it also reduced the number of skilled workers needed to build cars. Now 45 percent of line jobs could be learned within two to three days; 35 percent could be learned within a week. But sales dropped during the Depression. Only a million new cars were sold in 1932 compared with 4.5 million in 1929. Ford reacted by lay-

ing off workers and reducing wages and hours below those prevailing at General Motors and Chrysler. An Italian American auto-worker named Rizzo describes the effect employment cutbacks were having on his family:

I worka six years with this job, but all that time eight months is the longest I ever go steady in one year. For more than one year I only worka two or three days a week. Everybody say here, "Why don't you save when you worka?" But how can you save when you no worka stady? If I could get $5 a day all year, I could put this little pieca for the coal, this little pieca for the rent, this little pieca for the electric and maybe then I can putta this away for to save and know where I go. But now you work, you make something; you stop. You spend what you got save. You getta the debts. Then you get a job. You pay the debts. You save a little. You stop. And now I stop too long this time.[16]

To keep the men working, production lines in the Ford plant were sped up and bans against talking, whistling, and singing were sternly enforced. Working conditions, which had been difficult before, were now intolerable. The automobile industry as a whole had effectively resisted unionization for years by employing methods of intimidation and violence. Henry Ford, for example, took precautions to stop unionization before it could begin. He had microphones planted all over his factories and enlisted a factory police force, which he called the "Service Department." Hundreds of informants were placed on the production lines as well. The early auto strikes were among the bloodiest labor conflicts of the decade, second only to the conflicts in the mining industry.

The New Deal's National Industrial Recovery Act of 1933 gave a big push to the labor movement. It included a provision that gave employees the right to collectively organize and bargain. During the NIRA's short run of twenty-two months, the American Federation of Labor (AFL) moved quickly to rally labor in several different industries. AFL membership increased substantially during that period. In May 1935 the Supreme Court struck down the NIRA as unconstitutional. Congress filled the vacuum two months later with the National Labor Relations Act, also known as the Wagner Act, which offered stronger governmental support for unions. The act outlawed "unfair" practices employers had used to dissuade union activity, such as firing employees who are members of a labor union and for refusing to bargain during a labor dispute. The Wagner Act was a milestone for the labor movement because it put the power of the federal government behind the workers' right to bargain collectively and safely. The result was a substantial reduction in the number of deaths and serious injuries resulting from labor disputes. Union membership doubled and tripled now that employers could not use intimidation or strikebreaking tactics to delay or hamper negotiation. And industry did not collapse as was forecast by conservative opponents.

The worker won many victories during the 1930s that resulted in wage increases, job security, and reductions in working hours. Although tenacious union organizers were responsible for most of the inroads made, many people attributed the success to Roosevelt and the New Deal.

Life in the Country

During the First World War, from 1914 to 1918, American farmers had been urged to increase production; in return, the government guaranteed high prices and large purchases from other countries. Upon the advice of bankers, many farmers went into heavy debt, purchasing new acreage and investing in expensive equipment like gasoline-powered tractors. But when the war ended so did demand. Overproduction was the result, and large surpluses of cotton, wheat, corn, and other commodities sat unsold beside railroad tracks. Prices dropped so low that farmers lost money just harvesting their crops. Transporting them to market was yet another expense some farmers could not afford. While people went hungry in the city, food was rotting in silos on the farms. Thus farmers had been in trouble financially for years before the Depression started.

When the farmers could not pay their mortgages and loans, their farms were foreclosed and sold at auction. In the 1920s and 1930s, one in four foreclosed farms was sold. Many banks, however, were unable to sell farmland for a fair price. Groups of farmers banded together at foreclosure auctions around the country and bullied potential buyers out of bidding. They then bid pennies and nickels for equipment and property and returned everything to the original owner. Large corporations also took advantage of the depressed land prices and bought huge tracts of land for pennies on the dollar. In La Mars, Iowa, a group of farmers pulled a county judge out of his courtroom, put a noose

Unable to pay their mortgages during the Depression, many farmers lost their lands to bank foreclosure. Their equipment and property were often sold at auctions like this one in Hastings, Nebraska.

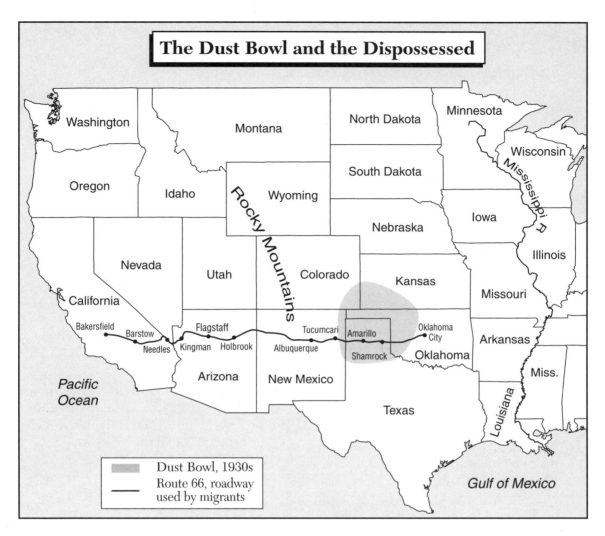

The Dust Bowl and the Dispossessed

Dust Bowl, 1930s

Route 66, roadway used by migrants

around his neck, and threatened to hang him for his insensitive handling of bankruptcy cases. The judge was released unharmed, but the incident was just one of many such confrontations to come.

Dust Bowls and Drought

From Texas to Canada, severe drought in the 1920s withered crops and dried the topsoil. Overgrazing by cattle and sheep across the Great Plains left no vegetation to hold the soil down. Further damage was caused by overcultivation and drought. The land became vulnerable to giant windstorms that blew the powdered soil into the air and left behind nothing but hard red clay and dunes of sand. Author Nathan Asch traveled through the Midwest interviewing farmers for a series of newspaper articles. One of his first trips was through the drought-stricken counties in Oklahoma:

I went inside the dust storm that for three weeks obscured the sun and made everything, food, water, even the air taken into

Even in the hardest times, most farmers could at least feed their families with a portion of their own crops or homegrown vegetables. But in the dust bowl areas where few crops survived the windstorms and drought, the farm wife had to be resourceful. Weeds have always been hardy plants that have survived herbicides, drought, and the trowel. Dandelion, cowslip greens, and lamb's quarters could be just as tasty as spinach when steamed and seasoned. In *Stories and Recipes of the Great Depression of the 1930's*, author Rita Van Amber recalls how her mother managed to keep meals on the table. Her family kept a sustenance garden that did not do well in the prolonged dry seasons. When everything else withered, weeds such as edible lamb's quarters prospered. Her mother canned and shelved the preserved weeds for the oncoming winter.

the lungs, taste gritty. It blew into the eyes, underneath the collar; undressing, there were specks of dust inside the buttonholes; in the morning it had gathered like fine snow along the window ledge; it penetrated even more; it seeped along the wiring of the house; and along the edges of the door button there was a dusty brown stain.[17]

The press called the afflicted areas "dust bowls" because of the large billowing clouds that blackened the sky for miles. The dust clouds swirled around the Great Plains, then traveled for hundreds of miles on jet streams and deposited dirt all over the south and in some parts of New York, Washington, D.C., and New England. The agricultural disaster thus created could not be remedied by policy.

A third of the population in certain counties of rural Oklahoma was unemployed and collected relief. In drought-stricken Arkansas, 150,000 families were on the verge of starvation when the overwhelmed Red Cross distribution line broke down. No food was given out for three days.

There Are Jobs in California

Large numbers of ruined farmers abandoned their land, now worthless, and let it fall into foreclosure. Some packed everything they could carry or fit onto their trucks and migrated west. Some hopped freight trains, took buses, or hitchhiked. Most drove in their own vehicles to California. Some came through Idaho and others traveled Highway 66 across New Mexico and Arizona. Those who took the southern route did not cross the large stretches of desert during the hot summer months, since their old cars and trucks were prone to overheat. By the end of the decade, an estimated 2.5 million people had moved out of the Plains states, making the dust bowl exodus the largest migration in American history. Over two hundred thousand people moved to California. The dispossessed southwesterners were largely illiterate and unskilled by California standards. Corporatized California farms utilized the latest technologies to harvest unfamiliar crops. Whereas in Oklahoma the largest crops were cotton and wheat, California farms grew fruit, nuts, and vegetables, but very little grain. As in John Steinbeck's important novel *The Grapes of Wrath*, about the Joad family's journey from Oklahoma, 40 percent of the migrant farmers moved to the San Joaquin Valley, where cotton was grown. The Oklahomans already understood the basics of harvesting cotton. They ended up picking grapes, pears, melons, peaches, and other fruits that required simple but different skills.

Go Home Okie

Once in California, many of the new migrants gave up their agrarian lifestyles upon discovering that the state's bountiful farmland was mostly controlled by agricultural monopolies. They moved into and around the urban areas in California and joined the legion of unemployed looking for jobs. The sheer number of them changed the cultural landscape of many California communities. Shacktowns called Little Oklahomas or Okievilles sprang up in open lots around cities such as Modesto, Fresno, and Bakersfield. Local landowners who had been sitting on undeveloped property came up with the idea of subdividing the land into small plots, which were sold for as little as $5 down and $3 a month, on the installment plan. Houses were built from scrounged scraps. Sanitation was nonexistent, as was plumbing, electricity, and police and fire protection. Available water was often polluted. Trash and waste were allowed to accumulate, creating a health hazard. Typhoid, malaria, smallpox, and tuberculosis broke out among the migratory workers.

The southwesterners sent their children to the local public schools and collected relief when they could. Over many years the shacks were replaced by real houses and the Little Oklahomas were absorbed into the towns they bordered. Urbanites were not happy to receive additional burdens on local relief, and they made life difficult for the new residents. Property taxes were increased to compensate for the rising costs of schooling and local relief. The "Okies" and "Arkies," as all the migrants were dubbed regardless of state of origin, were openly discriminated against by employers and harassed by police.

James Davis, the police chief of Los Angeles, took it upon himself to plug the flood of transients entering the state at the source. He sent 125 policemen eight hundred miles out of their jurisdiction to turn away anybody deemed undesirable at the Arizona/California border. This mission also gave LAPD an excuse to fingerprint the transients. The "bum blockade," as it would be called by the press, was not popular, however, with many citizens

After fleeing the dust bowl, migrant workers carried their belongings with them as they searched for work in California's farmland. Called "Okies" and "Arkies," these migrants faced discrimination by the local population.

of the border regions. Eventually the city attorney of Los Angeles questioned the usage of city funds for Davis's border patrol, and the officers were recalled.

Fifty Men for Every Job

Agricultural workers in California had always been ethnically diverse. The state's mild weather and lush rolling farmland attracted immigrants from all over the world. Although the state was predominantly white in 1930, it was the minorities who worked the land. In the nineteenth century, Chinese agriculturists had brought their unique skills into California and established the infrastructure of farming in the state. They hired themselves out to landowners to build canals and levees and to experiment with new crops. They eventually moved out of agriculture because of the limited opportunities available to them.

The Japanese followed, though they were not content to just work the land. They slowly struggled and worked their way into land-ownership through systematically acquiring long-term leases. By forming bargaining associations, the Japanese became very successful despite overwhelming prejudice. By the 1930s Japanese Americans owned or controlled 10 percent of California's agriculture. They became one of the few minority success stories

---

The Grapes of Wrath

The Grapes of Wrath *brought national recognition to author John Steinbeck, who is today heralded as one of the best American writers. His portrayal of the Joad family of Oklahoma became a national best-seller and won the Pulitzer Prize for fiction. But not everybody appreciated the realistic depictions of cruelty by California growers. The book was publicly burned by fruit growers and banned in California bookstores by local authorities who backed the growers. In this passage, Steinbeck describes the corporatization of farms in California.*

"And it came about that the owners no longer worked on their farms. They farmed on paper; and they forgot the land, the smell, the feel of it, and remembered only that they owned it, remembered only what they gained and lost by it. And some of the farms grew so large that one man could not even conceive of them any more, so large that it took batteries of bookkeepers to keep track of interest and gain and loss; chemists to test the soil, to replenish; straw bosses to see that the stooping men were moving along the rows as swiftly as the material of their bodies could stand."

John Steinbeck

The wife of a Mexican cotton picker washes her family's laundry in a tub outside her makeshift home. By 1930 Mexican migrant workers made up a third of California's total workforce.

of the period. From the 1920s to the 1930s, nearly thirty thousand Filipinos entered the state. They were known to be hard workers and accounted for 18 percent of the workforce. But the Mexicans surpassed them in number, becoming the largest immigrant group in California. Nearly half a million Mexican immigrants accounted for a third of the total workforce. Then in the 1930s local relief agencies began repatriating Mexican workers, sending more than 120,000 back to Mexico.

The southwesterners were the latest minority group to enter California and soon composed nearly half the state's migrant workers. They were accompanied by thousands of hoboes and former tenant farmers who had been driven out of the South by the Agricul-

tural Adjustment Act. The growers took advantage of this flood of workers by reducing wages. Those who were lucky enough to be chosen to work were temporarily boarded in sparse cabins with no facilities of any kind. Despite the low wages and miserable conditions, most of the farmers took the jobs without complaint. In most cases it was a better life than the one they had fled.

The southwesterners did not approve of unions or anything they perceived as being connected to communism. Upon their arrival, California was reeling from several years of violent union battles. The Cannery and Agricultural Workers Industrial Union (CAWIU), backed by the Communist Party, had organized some of the largest strikes in labor

Automobiles were prized possessions of migrant workers. In California, owning a car allowed workers to travel throughout the state to pick a variety of crops.

union history. These actions, in which up to fifty thousand workers had participated, successfully raised wages and improved working conditions. But the CAWIU was eventually weakened by organized groups of growers who used criminal syndication laws to jail the union leaders. This loss, combined with southwesterners' lack of participation, caused the power of the CAWIU in California to drop substantially.

On the Road

California led the country in farm mechanization. Because of the widespread use of tractors and other industrial machinery, fewer full-time workers were needed. Not all work could be done by machines, however; only human hands could pick, prune, and thin trees. California had a wide variety of crops that matured at different seasons, requiring workers to travel long distances to stay employed throughout the year. Thus the automobile was a most valuable possession. For migrant workers who earned piece rates (that is, were paid by each piece of fruit or vegetable picked), gas, oil, and parts were the most expensive overhead items. If the car or the maintenance money ran out, the migrants were stranded without a job, food, or shelter. Migrants often depended on the minimal camp facilities offered by growers. But when these were not available, whole families pitched camp on roadsides next to irrigation ditches.

Growers became concerned over the increasing number of poverty-stricken workers camped along roadsides. Rumors of strikes prompted them to take action to deter any kind of unionization. Following the pattern of California's long history of union busting, the growers lobbied for antipicketing ordinances and pressured local sheriffs to roust migrants out of their Hoovervilles. Bands of vigilantes beat up innocent men on suspicion of being communists, then burned their hovels to the ground.

California had an effective relief program in place for its own residents, but it was overwhelmed by the quarter million new migrants. The New Deal's Farm Security Administration (FSA) then built camps to temporarily house the displaced farmers from the Southwest. The FSA operated thirteen camps in California, which could service three hundred families each. These enclosed compounds of tents pitched on wooden platforms had communal showers and restrooms, and recreational facilities such as meeting halls and dance floors were available. There was a resident nurse in each camp, and when possible, a doctor was employed. Every human need was provided for, including the one that contributed to residents' self-esteem. The camps made people work for their room and board. Rent was charged, though it could be paid in chores. The community was self-governed by committees, allowing the residents to feel as if they were in control of their lives again.

Tenant Farming in the South

In 1930 over half of all southern farmers were tenant farmers who did not own the land they worked on. Tenancy was an outdated economic institution that evolved out of the southern plantation system. It allowed landless farmers to either rent a portion of land or work on parts of it in exchange for a share of the crop. The land the tenant worked was usually poor, and as a rule the plots were too small to yield a decent living. Even by Depression standards, tenants suffered more than other classes of people in the United States. Tenant farmer Donald Griffen recalls how the hard times affected his livelihood:

In 1931, like many other tenant farmers, I was heavily in debt, with my mules and most of my farm implements mortgaged. That year I made a "short" crop and was unable to "pay out." My creditors would show no mercy, and foreclosed, taking the

mules and most of my tools. All I had left, in the way of work animals, was two head of one year old steers.[18]

Tenancy existed all around the country but was the most prolific in the South and in cotton areas around the Mississippi Delta. In Arkansas, six out of ten farms were tenant operated, and in the Delta region tenants made up 80 percent of all farmers. Tenants fell into three classes: the cash tenant, the share tenant, and the sharecropper. Cash tenants owned their own animals and tools and essentially "rented" the land they farmed on. These farmers were economically in the best position to save enough money to buy their own farms. Between the cash tenant and the sharecropper sat the share tenant, who owned some tools but relied on the landowner to

With most of their money going toward food and housing, many people had no hope of bettering their situation during the Depression.

supply the rest. The share tenant paid a small portion of corn and cotton crops in rent; the rest was paid in cash. The sharecropper owned no equipment or animals and could offer only labor.

Sharecropping was the lowliest form of tenancy, and it evolved directly out of slavery.

The sharecropper depended on the landowner to supply animals, tools, food, clothing, and housing. In return, sharecroppers worked "halves," which meant they gave half their crop to the landowner, as rent. Dishonest landowners were known to divide proceeds unequally, so that most sharecroppers never

"I'se got strong hopes"

In this 1938 WPA account, interviewer W. O. Saunders describes a question-and-answer session he had with Mose Sutton, a seventy-year-old farmer from North Carolina.

"'How much do you make off your farm in a normal year?'

'Nothin', or almos' nothin',' he [Sutton] replied. 'If I have enough left over, after payin' for my go-ano [guano, fertilizer] and such, to buy flour an' meal and rise [rice] through the winter, den I calls myself lucky. I ain't made no money farming for ten or fifteen years. De landlord, he gets a fourth of de peas and de cotton and a third of de corn and sweet potatoes, and I gets the rest. He furnishes me a house, de outhouses and de land, and I furnishes the team, de work, de seed and de go-ano.'

'But how do you manage to live through the winter when you have a bad year like this?' I asked him.

'Well,' he replied, gravely, 'we just eats when we got anything to eat and goes hungry de rest of de time.'

When asked about his future, Mose responded:

'I can't get along much longer without some help. Me and my wife ain't got no children of our own here to home, but

we's raising four grandchillun, one four years old, one seven, one eleven and one fourteen. The fourteen-year-old boy does most of de plowing for me now, 'cause I just ain't able to do har work any more. But he'll be getting big enough to go off somewhere and work for somebody else, and den I reckon I'll jes have to give up farming. Folks jes don't want a tenant dat's wore out and can't make somethin' for them.'

'But what in the world would you do if your landlord decided to rent the farm to somebody else?' I asked, realizing that such an occurrence was not beyond the realm of possibility.

'Well, I'se thought about that,' Mose replied thoughtfully. 'I'se goin' to ask de landlord won't he let me have a little piece of land—about an acre—and if he'll do it I's going to build me a little house on dat piece of land and plant me a garden and try to git along somehow till I dies. Cou[r]se, it won't be much of a house. Jes a floor and a shingle roof and some weatherboarding, but it ought to keep out de rain and de sun and de wind.'

'What makes you think your landlord might give you an acre of land, Mose?' I asked.

'I ain't sure he'll do it,' Mose answered, 'but I'se got strong hopes dat he will.'"

Because of discrimination, black tenant farmers had lower annual incomes than their white counterparts.

made more than $100 a year (black tenants overall taking in considerably less than white tenants).

The housing provided to tenants was very poor. Units were typically unpainted one- or two-room shacks made of logs or corrugated metal and strips of wood, which let the wind and rain through. Mud was used in an attempt to plug the gaps between the slats, and newspapers lined the inside walls. Because these hovels offered little protection from cold weather and malaria-bearing mosquitoes, the death rate was high for infants and children in tenant families. Tenant houses also lacked modern conveniences such as electricity and indoor plumbing. Water was hauled in from nearby streams and ponds, which also were a source of food. The landowners ran stores where tenants and their families could buy food, clothes, and other necessities. Prices were marked up so heavily and landowners imposed credit terms so unfavorable that many tenants never received

any wages at all: everything they earned went to pay for the high-priced goods and credit. A third of all tenants moved every year in hopes of finding a more humane landowner.

The AAA's Unexpected Side Effects

Another of President Roosevelt's priorities upon entering office was to rescue the country's wallowing farming system. In 1933 he and his brain trust advisers drew up a radical piece of legislation called the Agricultural Adjustment Act (AAA). The measure sought to create a scarcity of food crops and cotton, which would in turn bring prices back up. The scarcity would be achieved by paying farmers to plow under a portion of their crops. A huge surplus of cotton was already flooding the market. Many desperate farmers took the offer and reduced their farming output by 25 to 50 percent. Prices rose to 10 cents a pound, but the plan had an unanticipated effect on tenant farmers. Because AAA subsidies paid 50 percent more than the market value for their crops and southern landowners made more money on their land through the AAA than through traditional arrangements with tenant farmers, most of the tenants were evicted. Then the landowners bought tractors and hired day labor to harvest the crop more efficiently and for less money. Some landowners took advantage of tenants eligible for part of the AAA subsidy checks by swindling illiterate farmworkers out of their share of the money.

Roosevelt reacted by pushing through the Bankhead-Jones Farm Tenancy Act of 1937, which evolved into the Farm Security Administration. Its objective was to get tenant farmers off the relief rolls by transplanting them to richer land and offering loans and grants with which to buy their own farms and equipment. The FSA also sought to teach these farmers how to maximize productivity on their new land. The FSA was surprisingly effective even though it was underfunded. Yet because of its minimal budget it could assist only one applicant in twenty-two.

Overall, the New Deal's agricultural recovery measures may have helped the landowners, but they offered very little consolation to the marginal farmer. For the 8 million sharecroppers who experienced unrelenting privation, no policy could offer a cure. The problem was more deeply rooted in the social fabric of the afflicted agricultural regions than in any political or economic reason—especially for black tenants. The discrimination and self-interest of local relief workers, farmers, and businessmen hindered the effectiveness of programs that might have hastened recovery or at least cushioned the blow of the Depression.

Life in a Mine Patch

The southern coal industry was another victim of overproduction. Hundreds of new mines had been dug and old mines reopened to meet the surge in demand during the First World War. By the end of the war, nine thousand mines were operating around the country. Demand dropped 50 percent, and prices plummeted. The availability of new and cheaper sources of power drove coal prices down even further. To save their profit margins, mine owners cut wages and "stretched out" working hours. In nonunionized coalfields, miners did not make enough to feed their families.

Mine sites were often dug far from established communities, so the companies built their own towns, which provided housing for miners and their families. The towns, called patches, were regulated by company officials in any way they saw fit. The company controlled every aspect of the employees' working and personal lives. The patch was a separate world with its own politics, laws, and police force. In Pennsylvania the company police were called the iron and coal police. Because of their remote locations, these organizations were recognized by the state as part of the official police force. The coal and iron police provided security for the mines, investigated theft and murder on the patch, evicted thousands of laid-off workers, and acted as strikebreakers. They were despised by the miners, who called them "yellow dogs" and "cossacks" for their heavy-handed methods of enforcing company law.

The Mining Town

Many of the miners were of eastern European descent (especially in Pennsylvania), but there was a broad mix of ethnicity. Also working in the mines were many southern blacks who had been brought in after World War I as "scab" labor to work for low wages when unionized workers were striking for higher pay. Everyone lived together in overcrowded, ramshackle "shotgun" houses (which were built with stacks of boards held together with nails shot from a gun). The houses had no utilities or indoor plumbing. Lighting came from kerosene lanterns or lard-oil lamps, and water was pumped outside and brought in. The screenless windows allowed coal dust to enter the house, staining everything. Employee housing was maintained at the expense of the tenant.

All miners grew their own food, since few made enough money to feed a family. Miners kept chicken coops in the yard and planted vegetable gardens in whatever open space was left. There was also the company store from which families could draw money against future paychecks to buy overpriced goods. Some miners called these commissaries "pluck-me" stores because the prices were twice what was charged in the towns. Anybody caught buying food or supplies elsewhere would be laid off, however. And if a decline in sales was noted, miners received a note asking what was wrong. Some patches paid wages in scrip to be sure of keeping all of the employees' business in the system.

If It Wasn't for My Family

Working in the mines was extremely hazardous. Coal mines were dark, damp, poorly ventilated, and full of rats. Even with support timbers, there was always the danger of cave-ins or explosions from pockets of natural gas. Miners were not paid for the time they spent erecting timber supports for mine roofs. To keep this "dead time" to a minimum, miners tried to complete the shoring-up work quickly and were likely to pay for their haste when the roof collapsed. Thousands died from cave-ins nationwide in the 1930s. Furthermore, air masks were not used in those days, so nearly all miners suffered from lung ailments. Breathing in coal dust could cause black lung, which severely reduced the lungs' ability to process oxygen. In Gauley Bridge, West Virginia, 476 miners died from inhaling silica dust over the mine's period of operation.

The miners' families were often the only motivation to continue working under such dreadful conditions. Families in coalfields were the largest of all industrial workers in

Armed guards like this one stood watch over mine workers and company property. These hired guns also enforced company law, which included forcing miners to buy goods only from the mining company's store.

the country. The isolation and oppression tended to pull families together. The wives of miners lived as hard a life as the miners themselves. Many times wives were summoned to mine entrances after a cave-in.

The children suffered the most. Growing bodies require regular meals, which were not the norm in the patches. Conditions were so poor in many patches that family members took turns not eating one day out of the week.

Schooling was a low priority, though the law required that children attend. School boards, however, were made up of mine executives who did not enforce the law. Miners themselves did not see any benefit from education and allowed their children to leave school at an early age so they could work in the mines. By law a mine worker had to be at least sixteen years old. There was, however, a provision that allowed the sons of miners to accompany them into the shafts. Thus many boys began working at nine or ten doing small jobs such as loading chunks of coal into the mine cars.

The Union

The United Mine Workers (UMW) wielded considerable power in the 1920s, when the union had 450,000 active members. In response to miners' demands, mine owners claimed they had to cut wages to survive. And mine owners had the full support of the local sheriff, deputies, and state militia to put down strikes at every opportunity. They employed every means possible to destroy the union, including violence and murder. The company police used spies to discover the locations of union meetings and waited in the shadows with saps and clubs to beat attendees. By 1929 membership was down to 150,000 and declining steadily.

The UMW was hurt by the Depression. Its strike fund had been depleted long ago, and members who were out of work could not count on any financial support. In the non-unionized coalfields of Harlan, Kentucky, tensions between miners and mine owners led to armed conflict. One of the main reasons for the tension in Harlan was the miners' complaints against the unfair practices of the company store. The store debited miners' paychecks for fuel oil and explosives they used on the job. The company even charged the miners blacksmithing costs to repair tools. Coupled with the overpriced goods that the miners were compelled to purchase from the company store, many workers actually owed money to the company at the end of each month instead of receiving pay. One miner wrote:

> We are half fed because we can'nt feed ourselves and family's with what we make. And we can'nt go to a Cut rate Store and buy food because most of all the company forbids such tradeing. If you got the cash. But now we have no cash. And the companies keeps their food stuffs at high prices at all time. So you can not clear enough to go anywhere. And if you do go some where and buy food you are subjects to be canned.[19]

In 1931, when the company scrip that was paid as wages dropped in value from 80 cents on the dollar to 40 cents, the miners spoke of joining the UMW. The company responded by posting armed guards to dissuade the miners from such thoughts. Even local politicians and judges were often in the pay of the mining companies and were thus unsympathetic to union organizers. Defying the authorities, and without endorsement from the UMW, the Harlan workers went on strike as an act of desperation. Another miner explained, "There

Relief Workers Were Not Above Prejudice

The effects of the Depression were even worse for black workers than for whites. Black workers' wages were lower, their hours higher, and their relief payments in many cases nonexistent because of discrimination at local distribution stations. In Down & Out in the Great Depression: Letters from the "Forgotten Man," *edited by Robert McElvaine, a desperate southern man anonymously appeals to the president for help. The letter is quoted directly from the source and the lack of punctuation in some places is inherent to the original.*

"Dear Mr. President

Would you please direct the people in charge of the releaf work in Georgia to issue the provisions + other supplies to our suffering colored people. I am sorry to worrie you with this Mr. President but hard as it is to believe the releaf officials here are using up most every thing that you send for them self + their friends. They give out the releaf supplies here on Wednesday of this week and give us black folks, each one, nothing but a few cans of pickle meet and to white folks they give blankets, bolts of cloth and things like that. I dont want to take to mutch of your time Mr. President but will give you just one example of how the releaf is work down here the witto [widow] Nancy Hendrics own lands, stock holder in the Bank in the town and she is being supplied with Blankets cloth and gets a supply of cans goods regular this is only one case but I can tell you many. Please help us mr President because we cant help our self and we know you is the president and a good Christian man we is praying for you. Yours truly cant sign my name Mr President they will beat me up and run me away from here and this is my home."

---

wa'n't nothing else for us to do. There wa'n't nothing to eat. No man could play shut mouth here and lie by himself alone and quiet. We was all marked. . . . It was time for a fight while we still could fight."[20] Clashes between the miners and guards and local police left four dead. The governor, who was also sympathetic to the company interests, called in the National Guard to quell the conflict, and he summarily ordered the arrest of twenty-eight suspected UMW members. Another union, the National Miners Union, stepped in to continue the struggle, but it was also expelled, thus ending union activity in Kentucky.

In other southern and eastern mines, however, union membership did take hold.

The National Industrial Recovery Act (NIRA) of 1933 guaranteed, among other things, labor's right to bargain collectively. This was an unprecedented victory for unions, and, furthermore, governors and other state officials were compelled to adhere to the government's codes. Union organizer John L. Lewis took advantage of the New Deal's prolabor stance to increase union membership. His campaign resulted in the formation of the Congress of Industrial Organizations (CIO) in 1935. Within two years the CIO had nearly 4 million members. The march to unionize was still slow and hampered, but workers continued to make significant gains throughout the remainder of the Depression.

Dropping Out of Society

Historians and economists agree that unemployment was the worst aspect of the Depression. It paralyzed business and drained cities of all of their resources. It put hardworking people who would never have considered accepting charity into breadlines and soup kitchens. Entire families descended into grinding poverty. As savings ran out and the charity of family and friends wore thin, the inability to pay the mortgage and make car payments inevitably resulted in foreclosure of homes and farms, and repossession of needed vehicles. In many cases even pawning what few belongings remained could not keep family members clothed, fed, and housed for the entire length of the pervasive economic dry spell. Desperate families resorted to taking relief, but the overburdened city systems had cut back payments drastically. Reporter Martha Gellhorn recorded what she heard from families forced to seek relief:

Their pride is dying but not without due agony. I get these comments constantly: We can't live on that $12 (family of ten)—we're going to starve and my husband can't find work—he's out every day looking—and I get afraid about him: he gets so black [depressed]. . . . If anyone had told us a year ago we'd come to this I'd have said he was a liar; and what can we do. . . . It's a terrible thing when decent people have to beg. . . . We always tried to be honest and decent as we could and we've worked all our lives; and what has it come to. . . . What's the use of looking for work any more; there isn't any. And look at the children. How would you feel if you saw your own kids like that: half naked and sick.[21]

Eventually such displaced families were forced to seek shelter in the cheapest housing they could find. They often ended up sharing space with other families in crumbling, overcrowded tenement buildings. When tenements were not available, Hoovervilles offered the only refuge for a family completely down on their luck.

Unattached singles fared worse than families during the Depression. They were perceived as being less needy and received proportionately less aid. Many single men left town on a boxcar and hoboed around. Single women roomed with other women in tenements if they could not find a place to stay at the YWCA or at a settlement house. Sometimes several women survived on the paycheck of one working roommate.

There Must Be Something Better in the Next Town

Hundreds of thousands who could not support themselves locally took to the road to find work. These mostly single men drifted from town to town and state to state, performing whatever odd jobs they could trade

During the Depression, many families moved west in search of work and a new life. These families often had to live in migrant camps with poor living conditions.

for food and a few coins. They became a familiar sight, hitchhiking along highways and hopping open railroad boxcars. The Southern Pacific Railroad reported that throughout the Depression its guards had thrown 683,000 people off the company's trains. There were so many transients that most railroad "bulls" (private police hired by the railroad) gave up trying to remove them. "Freight trains were amazing in those days," recalls garbageman Frank Czerwonka. "When a train would stop in a small town and the bums got off, the population tripled."[22] Some wives encouraged their husbands to leave home for the sake of the family, and not only to save on the food bill. Once the husband was away, the wife and children became "no-breadwinner families" who were then eligible for larger support payments from the government.

By 1932 there were estimated to be over a million people roaming the country. Many were Bonus Army veterans who had recently been chased out of Washington at bayonet point. Bonus Army members enjoyed prestige among other hoboes because they had shaken a fist at Washington, the perceived source of the country's misery. The fact that hoboes were unattached and continually moving made them targets for local police. In small towns especially, itinerants were rousted and jailed for vagrancy.

A quarter million wanderers were under the age of twenty-one. Most hobo minors were children who had dropped out of school to help support the family. But what few jobs were available to them in their hometowns paid very little and offered no security. They left to look for work in neighboring towns. And if they could not find anything, they moved to the next town on the next outbound freight train. The children of the road usually found the same bleak situation wherever they went, and some forgot why they left in the first place. Many continued to migrate aimlessly from city to city.

Poverty during the Depression splintered many families. The youngest children on the road often came from broken homes of divorce

thetic appearance to elicit sympathy when they panhandled. On the road they traveled in groups for mutual protection and company. A young hobo traveling alone was an easy target for criminals who either robbed them or used them to commit crimes.

What's a Woman to Do?

If jobs were scarce for men, they were even more difficult to obtain for women. Being married virtually eliminated a woman's chances of finding a job anywhere, since she was considered to have a source of income. Even school districts enforced policies of letting newly married female employees go. Thousands of unemployed women, unable to support themselves, joined the itinerant masses during the Depression. They cut their hair short, dressed in men's clothing to avoid being robbed or raped, and stowed away on the next freight train out of town. One of the most well known woman hoboes, Boxcar Bertha Thompson, rode the rails all her adult life. In her autobiography, entitled *Sister of the Road*, she wrote about the hundreds of hobo women she met during her travels:

> I've decided that the most frequent reason they leave is economic and that they usually come from broken or poverty-stricken homes. They want to escape from reality, to get away from misery, and unpleasant surroundings. Others are driven out by inability to find expression at home, or maybe because of parental discipline. Some hobo their way about to far away relatives, or go to seek romance. The dullness of a small town or a farm, made worse by long spells of the same kind of weather may start them off. But others are just seized with wanderlust.[24]

Hoboes followed the nation's rail lines, hoping to find work in the towns along the way.

and separation. Others were forced to flee from abusive parents or overtaxed social systems. Some were simply trying to relieve the burden on their parents. One fifteen-year-old girl named Kay attested, "There wasn't much else for me to do but go. There are eight younger kids at home and one older sister out of work. Dad hasn't worked steady for four years. Sis for two."[23] They took to the routines of adult hoboes and toughened quickly, however. They learned to beg and steal what they needed to survive, using their youth and pa-

Some women traveled alone, but most traveled in the company of partners. Often they traded sexual favors for food, money, transportation, or protection. Or, if they had no job prospects when they needed food or money, they conned local merchants or charitable organizations like Catholic missions and Jewish relief agencies. They slept in city parks and cleaned up in the jungles (hobo camps), in the restrooms of libraries, or in

The Wandering Bards

Tramps despised work. They would rather beg for scraps than earn a feast. They valued freedom over anything else. "Freedom is the one God I worship," proclaimed Harry Kemp, a tramp interviewed by a WPA writer. Harry Kemp, like many other tramps, was a poet and considered himself an artist. His compositions were recited around the evening fire in jungles along with other stories and verses. This Kemp ballad, from Roger Bruns's Knights of the Road: A Hobo History, *summarizes the difficult life a tramp can lead.*

The cars lay on a siding through the night;
The scattered yard lamps winked in green
   and red;
I slept upon bare boards with small
   delight,—
My pillow, my two shoes beneath my head;
As hard as my own conscience was my bed;
I lay and listened to my own blood flow;
Outside, I heard the thunder come and go
And glimpsed the golden squares of
   passing trains,
Or felt the cumbrous freight trains
   rumbling slow;
And yet that life was sweet for all its pains.

Against the tramp the laws are
   always right,
So often in a cell I broke my bread
Where bar on bar went black across
   my sight;

On country road or rockpile ill I sped
Leg-chained to leg like man to
   woman wed,
My wage for daily toil an oath, a blow,
I cursed my days that they were
   ordered so;
I damned my vagrant heart and
   dreaming brains
That thrust me down among the mean
   and low—
And yet that life was sweet for all its pains.

I crept with lice that stayed and stayed
   for spite;
I froze in "jungles" more than can be said;
Dogs tore my clothes, and in a
   woeful plight
At many a back door for my food I pled
Until I wished to God that I was dead. . . .
My shoes broke through and showed
   an outburst toe;
On every side the world was my foe,
Threatening me with jibe and jeer
   and chains,
Hard benches, cells, and woe on
   endless woe—
And yet that life was sweet for all its pains.

Brighter, in fine, than anything I know
Like sunset on a distant sea a-glow
My curious memory alone maintains
The richer worth beneath the
   wretched show
Of vagrant life still sweet for all its pains.

other public facilities. Many women were fastidious and tried to stay clean, since a dirty hobo was an easy target for police in the cities. But dirt, fleas, and lice were part of the life of being a hobo.

The Itinerant Classes

The public lumped all itinerants into a single group, but as in any community there were different classes. Just as there is an upper, middle, and lower class in standard economic jargon, there were hoboes, tramps, bums, and yeags. Each class represented a different lifestyle and attitude, not just a difference in names.

A hobo was a migratory worker who was hardworking and honorable—the working class of the road. According to St. John Tucker, former president of a hobo college in Chicago, hobo labor built the West. History shows itinerants to be an invaluable part of the labor force willing to live and work in the unsown wilds:

> Upon the labor of the migratory worker all the basic industries depend. He goes forth from the crowded slave markets to saw the forests, build and repair the railroads, tunnel mountains and build ravines. It is the labor that harvests wheat in the fall and cuts ice in the winter. All of these are hobos.[25]

There were hoboes who rose to great prominence. Before starring in the motion picture *Gone with the Wind*, actor Clark Gable hoboed around the country by rail. Poet Carl Sandburg and novelist Jack London wrote many well-known pieces about life on the road. Folksinger Woody Guthrie sang about his experiences, contributing one of the world's best-known ballads about the "hard traveler's" life:

I've been doin' some hard travelin',
I thought you knowd
I've been doin' some hard ramblin'
Away down the road. . . .
. . . I've been layin' in a hard rock Jail,
I thought you knowd
I've been laid out ninety days
Way down the road.
The darned old judge, he said to me,
It's ninety days for vagrancy,
And I've been doin' some hard
    travelin', Lord.[26]

Tramps, Bums, and Yeags

A tramp is a migratory nonworker who dreams and wanders. Unlike hoboes, who get restless when idle, tramps abhor any kind of work and prefer to beg or steal. It is a point of honor among tramps to stay unemployed and free. Although hoboes and tramps mixed in the jungles and the "Sallys" (Salvation Army facilities), they despised each other's lifestyle. Many young boys who grew up near railroad yards were lured into an itinerant life after hearing about the exciting, carefree life of the tramp.

A bum is a nonmigratory nonworker who cares only about drinking. Hoboes and tramps consider bums to be shiftless "booze hoisting" alcoholics. Bums have no desire to travel and prefer to stay close to home. Bums want to achieve comfort without working for it.

A yeag is an itinerant criminal also known as a grifter (con artist/thief), dip (pickpocket), or jackroller (mugger/thief), depending on his specialty. The word *yeag* comes from the German word *jäger* (pronounced yay-ger), meaning hunter. Yeags were always on the run from the law or other yeags. They preyed on fellow travelers and gave all itinerants a bad reputation. Tramps and hoboes avoided

A bum sleeps off his intoxication. While other itinerants were thrifty and eager to find jobs, bums had no desire to work and preferred the carefree stupor of alcoholism.

yeags as much as possible. Yeags have also been called Johnsons. Just as hoboes lived in encampments nicknamed "jungles," yeags lived in "Johnson families," where food and stories were shared.

Yeags frequently traveled with young protégés called "punks." The punks learned a craft like burglary or safecracking from the experienced yeag master or "jocker." Punks studied for years as journeymen apprentices, as did journeymen in any legitimate trade. One of a punk's main jobs was to case towns for places to rob. Punks masqueraded as tramps to allay suspicion while they checked out banks and post offices. Post offices were preferable to banks because of the low security and because the penalty for getting caught was not as severe as that for bank robbery. Upon successful completion of a job, the jocker and his punks vanished on the next freight train. Because of the number of itinerants continually coming and going in and out of towns, it was impossible for local police to track suspects once they had left the area.

Living in a Hobo Jungle

During hospitable months, open communities of hoboes sprouted along rail lines and were filled with whatever shelters could be hastily built with materials scavenged from the countryside. Hobo jungles were found near running water and at railroad intersections where several lines met. They also cropped up close to towns, where supplies and jobs might be found. They were called jungles because most were set away from the tracks in the tall grass and weeds. Some of the camps stretched for miles and offered a place to share a fire, some food, advice, and stories about life of the road. Many jungles were governed by a code of rules. Anybody caught breaking the rules, especially "jackrolling" (stealing) or wasting food, was subject to be stoned, beaten, and exiled. Jungles broke the race barriers that even the biggest, modern cities had not overcome. Black, white, Latino, and Indian shared food, supplies, and whatever intelligence could be gathered from local towns. Everybody was poor, but people tried to stay clean, and they cooperated to help each other find jobs and stock the Mulligan stew (a community soup made nightly of any food that could be scrounged).

Hoboes traveled light and survived only by improvising. Broken glass made a decent shaving razor, and flattened tomato cans served as plates. Forks and spoons were fingers, or pieces of wood or branches. Hoboes used kettles of boiling water to launder their clothing. They "boiled up" their clothes a piece at a time to kill any vermin hidden in the folds. Hoboes even had a clever way of keeping track of each other, as explained to a WPA interviewer: "The water tanks of railroads are the hotel registers of hoboland. Every bo carves his 'moniker' on the tanks and these registrations enable them to keep in touch with each other."[27]

Riding the Rails

The train was always the ride of choice for hoboes, yeags, and tramps: slow but free, for those with the nerve and agility to steal aboard freight cars. And the railroad reached every part of the country. It was also a symbol of allure and freedom for the adventurous and danger for the unwary. There are many accounts of hoboes who lost their grip and ended up under the wheels. A 1932 study by the Interstate Commerce Commission reported that 1,886 trespassers were killed by trains and 2,791 were injured. Legless or armless hoboes were not uncommon in the jungles. Railroad crews were another hazard of the rail that could deplete a hobo's hard-earned winter stash. Conductors and brakemen, or "shacks," were known predators in hobodom who shook down stowaways for "bo

money." Paying off shacks became a fixed cost for hoboes who failed to avoid being caught.

Hoboes who did not want to pay "bo money" had to be resourceful in choosing where to ride on the train. The most comfortable ride was also the first place the shacks checked, namely, in front of the luggage compartment or boxcar. The battery box beneath the passenger coach was uncomfortable but relatively safe from detection. Riding in a cattle car could be unpleasant and dangerous, since the livestock might violently crush a hobo against the unyielding slats of the car walls. The "reefer" (refrigerator car) was a good place to ride on trains traveling through the desert—unless a hobo got locked inside by a sadistic shack.

But the most daring hoboes rode on the cowcatcher at the front of the locomotive. "Cowcatcher" was the nickname for a pointed metal skirt mounted on the front of the locomotive designed to push aside animals that wandered onto the track and debris like tree branches. Riding the cowcatcher was extremely hazardous, since even a small stone could cause serious injury at forty miles an hour. But the smart hobo prepared by donning six or seven layers of clothing and a hat stuffed with socks for padding. Even then the shock and turbulence might pummel the most heavily armored hobo into unconsciousness. Anybody who survived to talk about the trip became part of an elite in hobodom. Author Roger Bruns writes of one hobo's close call with a cow:

Ahead the 'bo glimpsed an old white cow contentedly munching her cud. The wailing rush of the train brought little more than a blink from the cow but stark terror from the train jumper wedged up front. "I sort o' slid down on the back of my neck and h'isted my heels up in the air so's bossy would hit them first. Well, just before we reached her, she ambled calmly off the track, flickin' her tail."[28]

Another star in hobodom was the "trapeze artist," a hobo who rode underneath the car on part of the suspension. To accomplish this bit of acrobatics without getting killed

The Danger of Riding the Rails

Moving atop a moving train could be extremely hazardous for the hobo, especially if the hobo was being chased by a railroad detective. In Sister of the Road, *author Boxcar Bertha vividly describes the death of a companion who made a bad landing after a jump from the top of a freight train.*

"Jordan and I looked at each other questioningly, trying to decide whether to jump for it or not, and then I felt myself going—and reaching out—whether to save Jordan or to be saved by him, I don't know. And then the track came up to meet us and I felt

this terrific jolt which dazed me as I hit the cinders. I was conscious of the rumbling wheels of the freight train as they passed on and on endlessly, close to my ears, seemingly over my head, surrounding and terrifying me with their rumbling—conscious of the fact that I was holding onto Jordan's hands, which felt strangely heavy and lifeless, save for an intermittent, spasmodic, twitching. Then I became suddenly acutely aware of things again and saw that half of Jordan's body was on the right of way beside me and half of it was under the train."

Two hoboes catch a free ride on the top of a boxcar. Sudden jolts from the moving train, as well as pursuit by railroad guards, made the roof a dangerous perch.

A "trapeze artist" clings underneath a railroad car. Though the location helped hoboes avoid capture by guards, the undercarriage was a potentially dangerous place to sleep.

took a lot of dexterity and luck; but the undercarriage was the best place to avoid being caught by the shacks. The rod was a piece of the suspension that stretched between the cross-partition of the truck and the axle. Hoboes would swing their "ticket" (a wood plank with a groove carved down the center) onto the rod and lie on top. The ride was bumpy, dirty, and potentially deadly for a hobo who fell asleep and slipped off the ticket.

Moving On

The relief system and charities, which provided some comfort to the most needy, were themselves close to total collapse. American businesses, on the verge of ruin in these difficult times, could not employ the millions set adrift. In most cases, there was no place for people to go. It is not difficult to see why a million men and women left home for the road. This was especially true of former residents of small towns with limited relief re-

sources and a surplus of employable adults. The most logical recourse was to move on to another town where new opportunities might exist. When there was no job in one town, people would move on to the next and the next until they found something, even temporary jobs that paid just enough to allow them to survive for another few days without having to panhandle. And when that opportunity ended, there was always the next train out of town that kept them moving until they found themselves on the other side of the country.

On the road, people learned to reinvent themselves to fit their new roles. They adopted new customs and ways of speaking. These itinerant workers became a disconnected tribe of nomads who followed their own self-defined rules and customs. It seemed like a colorful life but it was a dangerous one filled with disease, hunger, and loneliness. But when there were no other opportunities available at home, many people preferred being on the road to sitting at home waiting for the next relief check.

5 Crime in America

I s it surprising that crime during the Depression broke records? Times were difficult, and disillusionment with the government and its laws was widespread. Prohibition proved to be a failure and left a new social phenomenon in its wake: organized crime. Gangsters like Al Capone and Dutch Schultz rose to infamy using violence and networks of bribery to control large bootlegging empires that rivaled any legitimate business in America. Capone's empire, which controlled over seven hundred men, including a few mayors and most of the police force in Chicago, offers a prime example of a large, well-organized criminal enterprise. Capone's estimated yearly earnings amounted to $100 million, which was an unbelievable fortune in 1930s dollars. Ironically, Capone's extravagances helped to

put him in jail. Diligent Treasury agents helped get the gangster convicted for tax evasion. An unsympathetic judge sentenced him to eleven years.

Kidnapping was another crime that was rampant in the early thirties. The Chicago police recorded two hundred kidnappings between 1930 and 1931 with ransoms totaling $2 million. The kidnapping of aviator Charles Lindbergh's infant son in 1932 became the most talked-about crime in the country. Lindbergh was admired for his contributions to aviation, archaeology, and medical research. A national hero, he was respected worldwide, as well. The case became a public preoccupation that was perpetuated by a continual news blitz. Thousands of telephone calls flooded police stations and newspapers from people who

Al Capone ran the Chicago mob in the 1930s. Though a notorious racketeer and bootlegger, Capone was jailed only for the crime of tax evasion.

claimed to have spotted the baby in a passing automobile or through a store window. Lindbergh paid the kidnappers $50,000 ransom, but the little boy was found dead six weeks later. German-born Bruno Richard Hauptmann was arrested and found guilty on largely circumstantial evidence. He was executed on April 3, 1936. After the Lindbergh baby was taken, incidents of kidnapping increased by 300 percent.

Despite the impact of these high-profile cases on the American consciousness during the 1930s, probably no single event created

Charles Lindbergh's infant son was kidnapped from the family home in 1932. Lindbergh paid the ransom, but his son was not returned. The boy was later found dead.

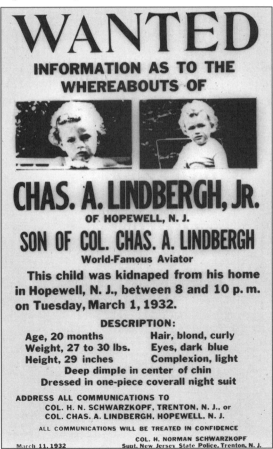

more criminals than Prohibition. The Eighteenth Amendment of the U.S. Constitution, backed by the Anti-Saloon League, the churches, and numerous other morality groups, banned the sale or possession of alcohol in the United States in 1919. Upon passage of the Volstead Act, which set up the machinery for enforcing this unpopular measure, people who otherwise respected law and order became closet drinkers, and an underground community of suppliers was created to serve them.

Prohibition: Failure from the Start

The Anti-Saloon League failed miserably in its attempt to force America to give up its favorite vice. Instead, the Eighteenth Amendment made criminals out of millions of men and women who, with little or no regret, flouted the Prohibition laws by patronizing underground taverns, or speakeasies, or brewing their own beverages at home. In Chicago, the police department estimated that some areas of the city had one hundred stills per block. The problem was just as bad in New York, where officials urged individuals with stills not to clog the sewers by dumping in such by-products of the fermentation process as soggy corn, grain, and potato peelings.

The lure of easy money was justifiable to people who regarded the law as unfair. Corruption became so widespread that everybody, from the neighborhood cop on the beat to the governor of the state, seemed to be on the take—and oftentimes this was exactly the case.

One of the most corrupt agencies was the border patrol, and it is not difficult to see why border patrol units were easily turned. Low morale and frustration prevailed in the ranks because of low pay and lack of proper equipment. There was a tremendous turnover, and

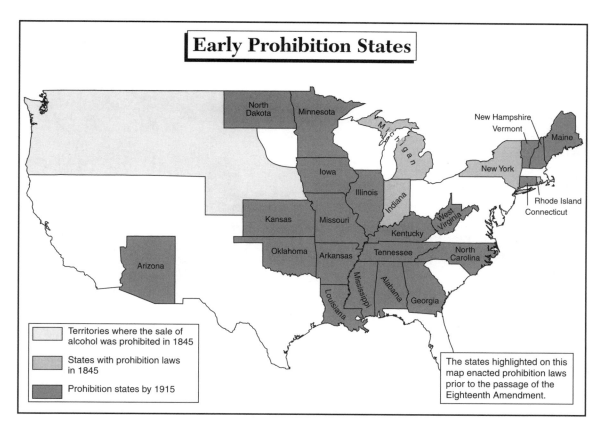

Early Prohibition States

Legend:
- Territories where the sale of alcohol was prohibited in 1845
- States with prohibition laws in 1845
- Prohibition states by 1915

The states highlighted on this map enacted prohibition laws prior to the passage of the Eighteenth Amendment.

many of the men who did stay in did so for the money coming from the other side of the law. Far better financed and organized, the bootleggers considered bribery an overhead cost, to be passed on to the consumer, who was forced to pay twice the price for liquor.

Eight years into Prohibition, Dr. James M. Doran, who had been appointed to head the national Prohibition effort, informed a congressional committee that proper enforcement would cost $300 million. Detroit, for example, was one of the biggest alcohol distribution centers in the country, deriving its endless supply from Canada, which was a short hop across the Detroit River. When Izzy Einstein, New York's number-one federal Prohibition agent, was invited to Detroit to help clean up violators of the Volstead Act, he left without much success, saying, "It would take the entire Prohibition force of the United States to dry up that place." [29] It was predicted early that enforcement would be difficult in large cities, but few had imagined how widespread the violations would be. It is now estimated that over the fourteen years Prohibition was in force, the federal government spent $370 million, and the state and local communities nearly $3 billion, trying to keep America dry. The $2 million originally set aside by Congress to enforce Prohibition represents a gross overestimation of the American people's willingness to quit a most beloved vice.

The Birth of the Rumrunner

It started with ordinary men and women opportunistically smuggling liquor from Canada in skiffs, fishing boats, and any other personal craft that would float. There were record numbers of water-craft license applications in Michigan during the first few years of Prohibition. For the price of a short trip across the Detroit River, a smuggler might make the equivalent of a year's salary. A single case of Canadian whiskey could be sold to a speakeasy in Detroit for ten times the original purchase price. Eventually well-organized combines took over most of the business on the river, setting prices and maintaining a loose code of conduct among rumrunners. There were plenty of "independents" who operated on the river, but those who crossed the combines were taken care of in a dark alley with a bullet.

The bootleggers were very innovative in their methods. It was rumored that rumrunners were using electronically guided, liquor-filled torpedoes and high-pressure pipelines. Neither high-tech system was ever uncovered, but customs inspectors did find some cables running underneath the Detroit River. A car was set on blocks in a fishing shack on the Canadian side, and its engine could pull a sled holding ten to twenty cases of booze underwater to the U.S. side. Bootleggers even used airplanes to smuggle an estimated $100,000 worth of liquor from Windsor, Canada. This was a fraction of what was being brought over by boat and train, but it was a unique use of what was then a novel method of transportation. It was also dangerous, and there were a number of well-publicized crashes. Because of the high cost and small amounts of contraband the planes could carry, the Prohibition bureaus stayed earthbound, instead relying on tips from local residents to discover hidden airfields. Irving Schleig, one of the best-known aerial smugglers, was legendary for his delivery record. He was arrested after crash landing in a field and was killed by his associates shortly after his release.

Officers seize a cargo of whiskey from a rumrunner's boat. Despite police efforts, the determination and innovation of the bootleggers ensured a steady flow of alcohol into the United States.

In the winter bootleggers drove cars and trucks over the frozen Great Lakes. The local police started to stake out popular pickup sites, but there was too much shoreline to cover effectively. Sometimes the police got lucky, and a slippery chase ensued over the ice, resulting in more than a few bruises for both parties. The bootleggers inevitably abandoned their vehicles to avoid capture, and some even wore ice skates to glide gracefully back to Canada. One group of bootleggers came up with the idea of using iceboats (sailboats equipped with skids to slide on the ice). Nothing the police had could catch the fleet iceboats, which seemed to capture the imagination of amused readers in the newspapers.

To the public, aggressive acts of law enforcement became as serious a hazard as violence from the bootleggers. Prohibition agents picked up the reputation of shooting first and asking questions later, and civilians were hurt or killed in pointless pursuits through the cities or across the lakes. Many honest residents who had houses and boats on Lake St. Clair, which separates the United States and Canada in lower Michigan, complained of being harassed by police patrols.

The Speakeasy

Disregard for the law became so flagrant that liquor was sold at well-known restaurants—by special request—and over the counter "by prescription" at drugstores. Steamship lines offered "wet" weekend cruises outside the twelve-mile limit. But the most common place to get a drink was the neighborhood speakeasy (the name derived from the way one would get in, by speaking quietly or "easy"). Indeed, there was no shortage of illegal drinking establishments in most big cities. During Prohibition there were estimated to be thirty-two thousand "speaks" in New York, twice the number of legal establishments that had been shut down. In Chicago there were more than twenty thousand. Speakeasies could be as simple as a single back room selling a home brew called "smoke" for 15 cents a glass to a full-scale nightclub with a bar, waiters, live bands, and a dance floor. Many brownstone buildings in Manhattan converted their basements into nightclubs, which were frequented by New York's society crowd.

The typical speakeasy customer was not a criminal, though criminals frequented and ran such establishments. The customers were as diverse as the cities. In New York you might run into Broadway producers, doctors,

A bootlegger's car dispenses a smoke screen to deter pursuing police officers.

lawyers, newspaper reporters, grandfathers and grandmothers, opera singers, and possibly a police officer or two. Even federal agents had their favorite places to go when off duty, and sometimes when on duty. But the most enthusiastic new patrons were women.

Women's Attitudes Change

Before Prohibition, no respectable woman was seen drinking in public, especially without her husband. After the Eighteenth Amendment passed and speakeasies started springing up across the nation, however, women flocked to the illicit bars in large numbers. There was immediately a substantial increase in women's drinking and drunkenness, and women began to smoke in public as well. In many New York clubs, the women were so much louder and more raucous than the men that some saloon keepers eventually banned women. Stanley Walker, a former city editor for the *New York Herald-Tribune*, recounts the adventures of Jim Brincker, proprietor of a speakeasy called the Nepenthe Club.

All over New York these up and coming females piled out of their hideaways, rang the bells of speakeasies, wheeled [persuaded] drugstores into selling them gin and rye, and even in establishments of great decorum [dignity] begged their escorts for a nip from a hip flask. It was all very embarrassing. Jim's corner place although he tried to keep a reasonable amount of decorum, could not escape the howling, reeling and raging termagants [overbearing women]. . . . When he opened the Nepenthe [his second club, after his first building was bought out by a bank] he announced that never, in any circumstances, would a woman ever be allowed to set foot inside the door.[30]

Speakeasy Lore

WPA writer John Colnon relates one of the many incredible stories told in speakeasies to patrons. The tale concerns Hank, a character who may have begun as a real individual but has since been built into a mythical figure like Paul Bunyan and Casey Jones. Hank is a wizard at mixing drinks that have peculiar effects.

"One night Hank was mixing up something for experiment. A few drops fell on the floor. There was a mouse running around under the bar. Suddenly the mouse reared up on its hind legs, roared like a lion and chased Hank and the bouncers right out of the place. Not long after, a pale man with a worried look asked Hank for a pick-me-up. Hank looked at the customer and remembered the mouse. He ran his eye over the array of bottles trying to remember what he had used. He took a little of this and a little of that with the air of an artist and the care of a drug clerk. 'Try this,' he said. But Hank never made that [drink] again. The little man coughed, whooped, turned a back somersault off the stool and got up fighting mad. 'Where's that cop?' he yelled and went out looking for the man on the beat. Soon the riot squad was out and when he finished up with them, the customer looked around, brushed his hands, and said: 'Now where can I find them damn Marines?'"

Women who were discouraged to smoke or drink in public enjoyed such freedoms behind the closed doors of speakeasies.

Repeal

On December 5, 1933, hundreds of thousands sat in their favorite speakeasies waiting for the Nineteenth Amendment to take effect, repealing the Eighteenth Amendment, or Prohibition. In cities across the country, police forces stood ready to guard against rowdiness. But the president had urged the nation not to abuse the freedom, and when word came down that repeal was official, America celebrated calmly and quietly. There was not enough alcohol to go around to every establishment, and legitimate breweries that had dusted out their vats and got the works operating were faced with a dilemma. Since beverage alcohol needs time to ferment and age properly, most of the alcohol that was immediately available through now-legal sources was not very palatable. The immature liquors were flavored to disguise their quality, which was inferior to that of many of the home brews and bathtub gins that were sold in speakeasies. The bootleggers' services were still in demand for quality alcohol from Canada and other foreign sources. The same operators also continued to run stills profitably. Several states had monopolized the liquor industry under their control, but bootleggers were able to undercut the official prices by selling illegally labeled wares through the back doors in alleyways.

During the Prohibition years, city patrons had grown used to the idea of having a local drinking establishment. Cocktail lounges, liquor stores, and bars sprang up in hotels and restaurants in large numbers in cities across the country. Many former speakeasies obtained

Famed bank robber John Dillinger (center) poses with prosecutors and other law enforcement officials after his arrest.

licenses to operate legally, and new nightclubs opened to big crowds. If it accomplished anything, Prohibition seemed to drop the barriers that divided the social lives of men and women.

Depression-Era Desperadoes

As times became more desperate, bank robberies in the Midwest skyrocketed. Marauders driving fast cars and packing Thompson submachine guns and sawed-off shotguns swept across the land, knocking off banks and post offices. Most of the robberies were committed by amateurs, but it was the charismatic Depression-era desperadoes like John Dillinger, Lester M. Gillis (known as "Baby Face" Nelson), Bonnie Parker and Clyde Barrow, George "Machine Gun" Kelly, and Charles "Pretty Boy" Floyd who stole the headlines. The press, in love with a handful of criminals, convinced America that the nation was under siege by a crime wave.

Pretty Boy Floyd became a legend by going on a crime spree that spanned three states.

He robbed so many banks in Oklahoma alone that the state's bank insurance rates doubled. Floyd's good looks, fine manners, and alleged generosity to anybody who helped hide him earned him a reputation as a Robin Hood among farmers in Oklahoma. Although officials pleaded with the public to turn him in, Floyd knew that a few dollars would buy him sanctuary at any farmhouse. His humble sharecropper beginnings made him more accessible and sympathetic to the common man than Al Capone, the Chicago gangster. Floyd became the country's antihero, glamorized in pulp magazines and comic books. He was killed in 1934 by FBI agents on an Ohio farm.

John Dillinger was the most well known bank robber of the time. He was an extremely intelligent individual who had a knack for shooting himself out of impossible situations. Dillinger escaped prison twice and always returned to what he did best, with his gang of bankbusters. His criminal career lasted only a year, but in that short time he managed to make the top of the FBI's most-wanted list.

Every police department in the country had Dillinger's photograph on the wall. To avoid capture, Dillinger had a facelift, grew a mustache, and used acid to alter his fingerprints. He was betrayed by a brothel madam and his girlfriend and was shot and killed by federal agent Melvin Purvis in front of a movie house, the Biograph Cinema in Chicago, in 1934.

The FBI

Before 1933, bank robbers simply crossed state lines to escape the law. Officers could make arrests in their own state only, and there was little interdepartmental cooperation between the police forces in the different states. In 1934 Congress enacted major anticrime bills that created six new federal offenses: kidnapping, robbing a federal bank, transporting stolen goods across state lines, racketeering, resisting arrest by a federal officer, and fleeing across state lines to avoid prosecution. Young J. Edgar Hoover revitalized the sagging reputation of the Bureau of Investigation, a do-nothing federal agency with no real powers of arrest, and changed its name to the Federal Bureau of Investigation. The FBI was granted limited powers over crimes that previously had been under state jurisdiction. The new charter also allowed FBI agents to carry guns and use any legal means to enforce the law. Bank robber Machine Gun Kelly is credited with dubbing the bureau agents G-men (government men).

As the FBI's crime fighting record improved, so did the reputation of its agents: Soon the tough and resourceful G-men were more admired than the gangsters. The G-men's exploits became popular radio fare and were splashed all over the pages of pulp magazines and comic books. Hoover himself was the focus of many stories, which spread the word of his accomplishments. For example, Hoover invented the crime laboratory, staffed by agents who used science to scrutinize crime scenes and evidence, and he implemented the use of a standardized fingerprint database for identification. Hoover also compiled a list of the top criminals in the country and set to work to rid the nation of its most dangerous enemies. Dillinger, Floyd, Nelson, and Ma Barker were a few of the most notorious figures on Hoover's most-wanted list who were tracked down and killed in bloody gunfights.

Rise of the G-Man

Early films had always portrayed the police as inept. But as the New Deal began to alter the

J. Edgar Hoover organized and headed the FBI during the Depression. Hoover and his agents attacked crime with a fanaticism that would eventually bring in many of the nation's most notorious figures.

public's image of government, Hollywood's depictions of law enforcement changed as well. Movies began to portray cops instead of criminals as the heroes. Well-known actors like Edward G. Robinson and James Cagney, who had always played aggressive, self-confident gangsters, now played aggressive, self-confident cops. In 1935 James Cagney, who earlier had starred in *Public Enemy*, playing a brutal gangster, played the lead in *G-Men*, a role that glamorized the FBI to millions of Americans.

J. Edgar Hoover despised Hollywood for its former tendency to glorify criminals, but it was suggested that he ended up helping filmmakers by acting as technical adviser during filming of *G-Men*, the first movie about the FBI. The producers used actual photographs of the FBI building to recreate scenes accurately. The audience saw the inner workings of the FBI, including the crime lab, the gym, and the machine gun ranges. The movie was well publicized by Warner Brothers, for the studio wanted audiences to think that seeing the movie was a patriotic duty. J. Edgar Hoover took an official stance that the FBI did not have anything to do with the movie. The Department of Justice put out the following press release on March 23, 1933, refuting Warner Brothers's claim that *G-Men* was an official record of the crime war.

It has been brought to the Department's attention that a motion picture newspaper has published an article stating that the department has designated a former agent of the Federal Bureau of Investigation to act as technical advisor in connection with various motion picture productions said to be in course of preparation on the Pacific Coast which purport to depict Department activities. Any statement in motion picture publications to the effect that the Department has au-

thorized any person to furnish technical advice or assistance is untrue. The Department has approved no motion picture scenario or production purporting to deal with its work.[31]

It was rumored, however, that Hoover had approved James Cagney for the leading role.

Junior G-Men

Children who in the past had fought to play the part of the gangster in make-believe games now fought to play the G-man. They were enthralled by the weapons, the high-profile cases, and the forensic techniques used to solve crimes. The roles were reversed, but the violent associations were the same, as shown by the following letter. Thousands like it were sent to Hoover from Junior G-Men clubs around the country.

Dear Mr. Hoover,

Please help me and my friends start an F.B.I. club. We need guns, bombs and other things to surprise the crooks. If you don't let us have this club, it would be like having a choice between law and crime, and saying you want crime.

Your friends,
Mickey, Herbie, Jeff, Ken[32]

Although Hoover did not allow the FBI to officially support this kind of publicity, he did everything he could to fan the flame: "The value of this sort of thing to the growing boy cannot be overestimated. He is taught that the policeman can be and is his friend, and he learns to see crime in its true light—as something far from glamorous, something sordid and evil that must be stamped out."[33]

Hoover Uses the Press

J. Edgar Hoover always understood the value of publicity. He was known to leak information on solved cases to the press. He accompanied agents on raids and always spoke on behalf of the bureau. FBI agents were never credited or mentioned by name, and they were never allowed to be photographed. Hoover became the FBI and spoke for all his men. This article, published on May 1, 1936, in the New York Times, *places Hoover in the forefront of the action.*

"Alvin Karpis, No. 1 bad man of the United States, was captured tonight without resistance by officers led by J. Edgar Hoover, chief of the Federal Bureau of Investigation. A few hours later the man who succeeded John Dillinger as the country's most wanted criminal, heavily guarded and manacled, was put aboard an airplane for a destination believed to be St. Paul, Minn. Without a shot being fired, though Karpis was armed, he was taken into custody along with Fred Hunter, 37 years old, a suspect in the $34,000 Garrettsville, Ohio, mail robbery, and a woman known only as 'Ruth,' as they emerged from an apartment building about half a mile from the center of the business district. Mr. Hoover made the announcement with the simple statement: 'We have captured Alvin Karpis, generally known as Public Enemy No. 1. He was taken without the firing of a shot. Karpis never had a chance. There were too many guns on him.'"

Advertisers took advantage of the nation's fascination with G-men by organizing clubs and promotions, which they linked to movies, radio shows, and magazines. Breakfast cereal companies promoted detective clubs. Quaker Puffed Rice had Dick Tracy's Secret Service Patrol, Post Toasties had Inspector Post's Junior Detective Corps, which was renamed the Melvin Purvis Law and Order Patrol after the FBI agent who had gunned down Dillinger. All a boy or girl had to do to join was to eat lots of cereal and redeem the box tops for a detective badge and a cluebook containing a "secret password" that only detectives knew. Imaginary cases were printed on the back of cereal boxes.

Bubble gum manufacturers created G-man collectible bubble gum cards with condensations of actual FBI cases on the back. Some of the manufacturers offered series of numbered cards but skipped some numbers so kids would keep buying, in the belief that they were missing items designated by the unused numbers.

It was all part of Hoover's plan to elevate the reputation of the FBI above that of the criminals it pursued.

CHAPTER 6

Escaping the Great Depression

During the Depression many people found themselves with a surplus of free time. Businesses across the country reduced wages and cut back on employee working hours in an effort to survive. Six- and even seven-day workweeks were being supplanted by the five-day week. With weekends and evenings free, the working class had more time for entertainment and leisure. Hundreds of fads, gimmicks, and preoccupations possessed the American people in the 1930s.

After the stock market crash in 1929, the radio business—unlike most other businesses—prospered during hard times. Television, which would have a similar effect years later, was not yet ready for the general public: the technology existed on a basic level, but there was a lack of compatibility and standards among developers. Also the low quality of the picture kept the television out of the hands of all but the wealthiest novelty seekers for another ten years. But of all the inventions that came and went, none rivaled the radio in popularity. Herbert Hoover called it "an instrument of beauty and learning." Even among the unemployed and the homeless, radio played an important part in people's lives. Radio provided cheap entertainment and brought the latest news and world events into the home in real time. Popular modes of thinking and living were created by radio. The ways in which Americans ate, dressed, played, and spoke were influenced by radio programming and advertising. No longer would city dwellers alone know the latest song or saying. Farmers in rural Iowa and Nebraska listened to the same programs and commercials as people in Manhattan and Detroit.

A Member of the Family

Radios during the 1930s were far from the compact and portable units that fit in the pocket today. Some early radios were housed in formidable pieces of furniture made of wood

Radio linked people to the news and events of the day. It also helped to offset the bleakness of the Depression with hours of entertainment programming.

or Bakelite (an early plastic). The working parts were rows of fragile glass vacuum tubes that glowed when operating. Radios came in many different shapes, however, suitable for table-tops as well as for cars. The popular console radio was designed with cascades of tubular trim, to fit smartly into the decor of the 1930s living room. Sets were made by Zenith, Silvertone, Belmont, and Arvin and sported names like Rhythm Maid and the Freshman Masterpiece. Despite its high cost (an average of $100 in 1929), a real tube radio became an indispensable fixture in the lives of 12 million Americans. It was also a phenomenal sales success. In 1929 manufacturers were barely keeping up with demand, selling $852 million worth of receivers. It is estimated that 85 percent of the country, or 28 million people, owned at least one radio set in home and car by 1939.

Father Charles Coughlin lit up the airwaves with his sermons. A staunch conservative, Coughlin often used his broadcasts to attack the liberal policies of President Roosevelt.

Radio Clutter

The number of radio broadcasters expanded greatly during the 1920s and 1930s. But because radio was such a new medium, no regulations had been written to control what went out over the airwaves. Radio stations frequently broadcast over each other and created static-filled confusion. Astrologers, soothsayers, and quack psychologists flocked to buy airtime and added to the clutter. Dr. J. R. Brinkley, the infamous "goat gland man," was an on-air shyster who peddled cure-alls of his own devising that made use of exotic ingredients. In a year he was barred from practice for quackery and silenced by a new regulatory agency, the Federal Communications Commission, which was established in 1934.

The magnetic Irish-Canadian radio messiah from Michigan, Father Charles Coughlin, was another colorful character of Depression radio. Father Coughlin was a Roman Catholic priest whose angry sermons were more political than spiritual. He attacked communists, Jews, labor unions, and big business. His program was broadcast on sixty stations and attracted an estimated 30 million loyal listeners. Tens of thousands of letters were received daily in response to Coughlin's heated sermons. Many people sent checks to his radio program. Coughlin eventually launched a political party, the National Union for Social Justice, which tried to get William Lemke, a congressman from North Dakota, elected to the White House in 1936. But even Coughlin's considerable influence had little effect on election day, and Lemke's disappointing total was no more than a million votes. President Roosevelt was handily reelected, and the Social Justice Party's defeat made Coughlin more militant than ever.

Coughlin was one of President Roosevelt's fiercest critics. In a 1935 broadcast Coughlin accused "Franklin Double-Crossing Roosevelt" and his New Deal of embracing socialism:

President Roosevelt has both compromised with the money changers and conciliated with monopolistic industry. This spirit of compromise has been the predominant weakness of our present leadership to such an extent that it has not disdained to hold out the olive branch to those whose policies are crimsoned with the theories of sovietism and international socialism. We cannot applaud a New Deal which, with all its chaotic implications, submits either to the supremacy of a financial overlord more obnoxious than King George III or to the red slavery of an economic Simon Legree [the cruel slave driver in *Uncle Tom's Cabin*].[34]

Coughlin was forced by his archbishop to apologize on the air for unflattering remarks to the administration, but he returned to lambasting the president the following week. Eventually Coughlin's popularity waned as his listeners began to tire of his thinly disguised pro-Nazi and anti-Semitic rantings. He and his followers, the self-proclaimed Christian Front, were completely removed from the airwaves by the church in 1942.

What They Listened To

The radio brought live music into the homes of American listeners. In the 1920s, classical music programming was the most common broadcast, followed by sportscasts and radio plays. By the 1930s popular music surpassed classical as the most listened-to format. Radio popularized many new forms of music, including crooning, the singing cowboy, ballads, and swing. Big bands and swing came of age in the late 1930s. Swing was a watered-down version of the hot jazz played in the 1920s. Jazz is a free-form way of playing; swing is

Nothing Split Five Ways

Even the entertainment industry had a difficult time during the 1930s. Leo Walker was a trumpet player in a swing band during the Depression until an auto accident ended his career. In his book The Wonderful Era of the Great Dance Bands, *he describes the low-paying gigs he and his band took to pay the bills during hard times.*

"We had trouble getting 50 percent of a sometimes fast count box office take. A top admission price would be fifty or seventy-five cents, and this was a rare occasion; in most instances the charge was twenty-five cents for a whole evening's dancing. The all-time low came one stormy Saturday night in northern Kansas when we drove ninety miles to the job, played four hours, and split up the pay-off at ninety cents each for the evening's work after expenses were deducted."

more structured. Both have a strong beat and powerful, unencumbered rhythms. Swing derives its name from the free and loose nature of the music.

The radio also popularized situation comedies and dramas. Of all the radio programs broadcast during the 1930s none ever achieved the fanatical reach of *Amos 'n' Andy*. Radio was changed forever by the show's stars, two former vaudeville actors, Freeman Gosden and Charles Correl. They were white performers whose on-air characters used an exaggerated black dialect and, in the story line, worked for the Fresh Air Taxi Cab Company.

The National Association for the Advancement of Colored People (NAACP) complained to the FCC about the negative stereotypes portrayed in the show, but broadcasting executives were quick to point out that many blacks enjoyed the program as much as whites. Over 30 million people, including the president of the United States, tuned in to *Amos 'n' Andy* from Monday through Friday. Only fifteen minutes long, the program quickly became the most popular radio comedy in history. Movie houses advertised on their marquees that they would stop midreel to pipe in the daily broadcast of *Amos 'n' Andy*. Department stores aired the show for shoppers, and traffic across the nation was known to stop as people pulled over to switch stations or abandon their cars for the local radio shop. A person could walk down any street in America at seven o'clock and hear the sounds of *Amos 'n' Andy* coming out of one window after another.

The true power of the airwaves, however, was demonstrated on a bleak Halloween in 1938, when CBS's *Mercury Theater of the Air* broadcast a drama based on *The War of the Worlds*, a novel by H. G. Wells. The plot centered on the invasion of Earth by Martians, and the script was written to give the impression that such an invasion was actually occur-

ring. To lend authenticity to the broadcast experience, producers Orson Welles and John Houseman inserted phony news bulletins between musical programming and weather reports. Thousands of calls poured in to CBS, to newspaper offices, and to the police from panicked listeners who thought the world was ending. Roads were clogged as people tried to flee. Families in Newark rushed out of their houses with wet towels over their faces to protect themselves from the poison gas raid that was portrayed. CBS made special announcements all night after the broadcast to reassure listeners that it was just a joke, but the excitement did not completely subside for weeks. Shortly afterward, the Federal Communications Commission conducted hearings and passed regulations banning fictional news broadcasts.

Orson Welles and John Houseman were not the only people to use the power of radio. President Roosevelt immediately recognized the potential to reach a large audience and used radio to rally the nation. He often spoke directly to his constituents, using a friendly and informal tone. These speeches, known as

Freeman Gosden and Charles Correl provided the voices for the title characters on radio's Amos 'n' Andy. *The show was the most popular broadcast during the Depression, attracting 30 million listeners each week.*

Franklin Roosevelt's fireside chats kept Americans informed about his plans to speed economic recovery.

"fireside chats," had a remarkable calming influence on the nation. In his first fireside chat, Roosevelt discussed his plans to stabilize the banks. The following day deposits exceeded withdrawals nationwide. Several days later, the stock market rose 15 percent, its largest one-day increase in history.

There's Always Room in the Budget for a Movie

Second only to radio, movies became a very popular form of entertainment during hard times. Movie houses saw a sharp drop in attendance in the beginning of the Great Depression. But the setback was only temporary. Bingo, double features, and prize drawings were some of the marketing gimmicks owners used to attract viewers back. Although money was tight, people managed to scrape together the dimes and nickels needed to see the latest Clark Gable or Shirley Temple film. Few could afford luxuries in real life, but they could find enjoyment by watching the characters on-screen, who wore expensive suits and

gowns and lived in extravagant apartments and houses. Movies fulfilled a deep need.

In the beginning of the Depression Hollywood felt the effects of the economy the same as did all other industries in America. But soon box office receipts returned and far exceeded the numbers of previous years. Movies became a prosperous industry during hard times. Film and stage actress Myrna Loy recalls how insulated Hollywood seemed to be from the rest of the world. "When the Depression came, I had a very good job in Hollywood. It was just at the beginning of my career. It was really distant to me. Everybody around me was working."[35]

By 1929, the silent film was dead in America. Sound gave new realism to film not only by adding dialogue but also by regulating the speed of movement, which had to be synchronized to the actors' speech. Color soon made its debut, as well, in Disney cartoons. In its infancy, the Technicolor process produced films in which the colors seemed to be applied by the inking methods used in comic books. *Becky Sharp* (1935) was the first full-length movie to utilize Technicolor. Four years later,

Radio Panic

A large part of the country became convinced that the world was ending during Orson Welles's War of the Worlds *broadcast largely because of the steps he took to make the fictional events appear to be authentic. Here is a transcript of the broadcast, taken from* This Fabulous Century: Sixty Years of American Life, *showing how Welles and actor John Houseman interrupted segments of supposedly regular programming (here represented by Announcer 1) with fake news flashes (as in the words of Announcer 2).*

"Announcer 1. Good evening ladies and gentlemen. From the Meridian Room in the Park Plaza in New York City, we bring you the music of Ramon Raquello and his orchestra. With a touch of the Spanish, Ramon Raquello leads off with 'La Cumparsita.'

Announcer 2. Ladies and gentlemen, we interrupt our program of dance music to bring you a special bulletin from the Intercontinental Radio News. At twenty minutes before eight, central time, Professor Farrell of the Mount Jennings Observatory, Chicago, Illinois, reports observing several explosions of incandescent gas, occurring at regular intervals on the planet Mars. The spectroscope indicates the gas to be hydrogen and moving towards the earth with enormous velocity. Professor Pierson of the observatory at Princeton confirms Farrell's observation, and describes the phenomenon as like a jet of blue flame shot from a gun. We now return you to the music of Ramon Raquello, playing for you in the Meridian Room of the Park Plaza Hotel, situated in downtown New York."

Orson Welles (center) was a well-known radio dramatist who eventually transferred his talent to acting in and directing films.

Margaret Mitchell's best-selling novel *Gone with the Wind* was filmed in Technicolor and broke theater records, giving the biggest push yet to the new technology. After the incredible success of *Gone with the Wind*, every studio started to produce color films.

Comedies and lavish musicals, which coincided with the optimism of the New Deal, were also popular escapist fare, and Hollywood cranked them out by the carload. The irreverent Marx Brothers made their debut in the 1930s. Groucho, Chico, Harpo, and Zeppo were former vaudeville comics who brought their act to the screen. Using a flurry of sight gags and rapid plays on words, the quartet captured audiences with ten years' worth of hit comedy movies. *Duck Soup* (1933), *A Night at the Opera* (1936), and *At the Circus* (1939) were among their best. Mae West was a Broadway import whose quips about sex sent audiences into hysterics. The suggestive nature of some of her one-liners shocked many social critics of the day. W. C. Fields was another of movie history's greatest comic characters. Much of the comedy was derived from Fields himself, as opposed to the story. His red nose, beer belly, and posturing were part of his unique personality, a personality that has often been borrowed by comedians throughout the years.

What They Read

Like the movies, books and magazines were a perfect low-cost diversion to take people's minds away from domestic problems. Library patronage shot up during the Depression, though many of those who occupied seats in libraries were homeless people looking for a dry place to stay. Despite their considerable heft, Hervey Allen's *Anthony Adverse* and Margaret Mitchell's *Gone with the Wind* were wild successes that broke sales records. *Gone with the Wind* sold a million copies in the first six months. Pearl Buck's story of peasant life in China, *The Good Earth*, won the Pulitzer Prize in 1932; the author donated all her royalties to local relief funds. Self-help books also sold well, including Dale Carnegie's *How to*

Mae West and W. C. Fields costar in My Little Chickadee. *Both actors had outrageous personalities that brought them great fame and harsh criticism.*

Win Friends and Influence People and Dorothea Brande's *Wake Up and Live.*

Newspapers lost readership to radio and movies. The slick magazines such as *Life, Fortune,* the *New Yorker,* and *Colliers' Weekly,* however, did well. Many of the leading magazines featured work by America's literary elite: Ernest Hemingway, William Faulkner, F. Scott Fitzgerald, and Willa Cather. The MacFadden publishing group produced several popular magazines, including *True Stories, True Romances, True Ghost Stories,* and *True Lovers.* The scandalous stories were supposedly drawn from the "true confessions" of readers.

But it was the comic strips, comic books, and pulp magazines that achieved overwhelming success during the Depression. Comics were not new to newspapers, but adventure strips became the favorite fare of Depression readers. *Buck Rogers* (1929), *Tarzan* (1931), and *Flash Gordon* (1934) were a few popular titles that transported readers to exotic places. The lives of America's young circled around these adventure characters, who were also featured in movies and radio programs. Comic books evolved out of the comic strip and were read by children and adults.

Comic Strips Were Not Always Funny

Little Orphan Annie, by Harold Gray, was one of the most popular strips in the 1930s. It was the first adventure comic that featured a female hero. Orphan Annie explored the major problems of the Depression: unemployment, labor unrest, corruption, and organized crime. The story followed red-headed Annie, an orphan adopted by wealthy socialite Oliver Warbucks. Annie was good-natured, accepting, and indifferent to material wealth. War-

bucks, a self-made man, was strong, ambitious, and independent. After a few uncertainties as each adjusted to the other's strong personality, the two became inseparable. Throughout the initial series run, Annie and Warbucks were afflicted by a series of catastrophes. Artist Harold Gray subjected Warbucks to the financial disaster every American businessman had faced during the Depression. Warbucks lost several fortunes but always rebuilt his empire, using nothing but hard work and initiative. Even after going broke and losing his sight in the series, Warbucks refused any kind of charity. In Warbucks's success, Gray created a simple formula for America to follow. It was a message to the public that people could find work if they were not choosy. And by working hard, they could succeed no matter how difficult the conditions were.

Born on a farm in the Midwest, Harold Gray was raised to value hard work and self-reliance, the qualities that motivated all his characters. He was very much against labor unions and any kind of relief. Gray's strip continually attacked Roosevelt's New Deal programs, which he considered to border socialism. Gray and his wife traveled around the country talking to people and asking their opinions on relief, the economy, and a wide variety of subjects, and he used the responses to build his strip.

Pulp Magazines

The thirties enjoyed a renaissance of pulp magazines, which represented escapist fiction at its very best. The periodicals derived their name from the cheap paper they were printed on. Pulps, costing anywhere from a nickel to a quarter, attracted a readership of millions. The broad and inventive subject matter included westerns, mysteries, science fiction, and any combination of genres that would make an interesting story. The magazines also featured pages full of ads selling cure-alls, methods of self-improvement, and money-making schemes. The covers were splashy and often risqué, portraying scantily clothed, vulnerable women being threatened by masked villains or giant spiders.

The successful pulp writer produced prodigious amounts of text. Sometimes writing one or two stories a day was the only way to make money. Ideas were drawn from real experiences in everyday life or borrowed from other writers. All a writer had to do was change the time, place, and genre to go from a showdown at the O-K Corral to a showdown in space. The writers were an eccentric but varied group of people from all fields. Former journalists, convicts, cowboys, and teachers flocked to New York to personally submit their work to the many publishing houses.

Comic books and the pulps were accused of perpetuating juvenile crime and delinquency and of lowering educational standards. But in actuality the pulps helped to perpetuate literacy. As far back as the nineteenth century, pulps brought casual reading to people who did not have much education. Combined with advances in printing technology (which allowed large quantities of printing at affordable prices) and expanding postal services (which provided a broader range of distribution), the pulps reached deep into the heart of America.

Other Diversions

Even through the boom or bust years, the American people came up with ways to test themselves in ludicrous ways. Whether swallowing a dozen goldfish, sitting on a flagpole or in a tree for several weeks, or dancing in a marathon for several months, there was something new passing in and out of popularity every day. Some of the more enduring fads attracted thousands of copycats around the country, willing to drop everything to achieve an instant of fame. If riding a bike in circles for 13 days did not get a person noticed, then playing the piano for 240 hours would. The 1930s will forever have the distinction of being the decade of fads.

One of the most popular fads was the marathon. Marathons of every imaginable type were scheduled: There were walking, running, talking, and drinking marathons, and even kissing marathons. A United Press survey described this new national obsession as pastimes for a nation of crazies. Dance marathons were the most brutal of marathons. They promised temporary fame and big prizes to anybody with a little talent and a lot of desperation. The events were advertised by promoters as contests open to anybody, but many of the contestants were professional marathoners who were paid by promoters to keep the audience interested. Hundreds of people looking for easy money entered the contest. Most of them ended up dropping out after the first few weeks, as a result of exhaustion or sabotage by veteran dancers.

Dance marathons were held in stadiums and large arenas with plenty of seating. They were advertised all over town, and the music and announcements of the contestants' times were broadcast on the radio. Spectators paid a quarter to watch their favorite couple drag their sleep-deprived bodies across the floor. The aim of the competition was to outlast other dancers in an exhibition of dancing with a minimum amount of rest. The routine at most marathons was the same: Contestants danced for an hour to a mix of fast and slow songs. At the end of the hour couples retired backstage (their only scrap of privacy) for eleven minutes of rest. Showers and cots were available in two large rooms, which were shared by men and women, and laundry was taken care of by the promoter for a fee. Swedish masseuses were employed to keep dancers' muscles limber, and nurses waited on the sideline to assess the likelihood of total collapse as competitors neared exhaustion.

At the end of every rest hour loud sirens called the dancers back to the arena for another session. A smorgasbord of high-calorie meals was wheeled atop gurneys into the arena every few hours, and contestants ate while dancing. Many dancers learned to eat just enough to re-plenish their energy until the next feeding,

A sleeping dancer is lugged around by her part-ner during a dance marathon.

since overeating caused drowsiness. This cycle was repeated twenty-four hours a day and lasted anywhere from a week to five months. The health department of the host cities often intervened when conditions deteriorated.

A good partner was critical to surviving, since contestants relied on partners to carry or "lug" them around the dance floor, a practice that allowed the pair to sleep on their feet, in shifts. Binding hands behind a partner's neck was a common tactic couples used to survive after a few hundred hours of dancing.

When attendance was down, promoters often introduced new twists to spark interest. Sprints and grinds were elimination tech-niques guaranteed to narrow the field in a dazzling way. Periods of frenzied dancing or "sprints" around the floor were made more difficult and entertaining when contestants were tied together.

Dancing was only part of the total attrac-tion of the marathons. From the beginning, the promoters looked for performance talent in contestants. The dance marathon was actu-ally a cross between a musical stage play and a circus. Everybody involved, including the nurse, the janitors, and the promoter, was constantly on display. Many contestants and couples had acts they would perform on re-quest by audience members. If they pleased the crowd, they were rewarded with a shower of coins. Comedy and drama were staples of the dance marathon. Every failure, as well, was shared by the audience under the spot-light. When a dancer was hurt, he or she was brought to an onstage "hospital" to be treated by the nurse.

Actress June Havoc is considered to be one of the all-time marathon champions, hav-ing set a thirty-six-hundred-hour dance record while lugging her partner, Elmer "Sparkplug" Dupree. In her book *Early Havoc* she de-scribes how she felt:

Of course you were always on the verge of falling down, the way you did when you're untrue to your system, but you kept going somehow. The sound of the band or the scratchy old phonograph records amplified a hundred times in those tinderbox arenas and rollerdromes helped to keep you going when you were dragging. The audience helped you too.[36]

Rising to New Heights

Simply sitting on flagpoles and in trees was another craze that gripped the nation during the 1920s and 1930s. Thousands of children indulged in the sport, to the distress of their concerned parents. Reports of children who broke arms and legs falling out of trees prompted cities to assign police patrols to rove the city and keep people grounded.

Professional flagpole sitter Alvin "Shipwreck" Kelly is considered to be the founder of this strange movement. He got his start when he was thrown out of a third-story window by a group of overzealous boxing fans. He hit a flagpole and hung on for dear life. Later, Kelly amazed audiences around the country in what became for him a full-time job (he was estimated to have made as much as $29,000 in one year for endorsements). He charged $100 a day to break every record sitting on his perch—a modified automobile brake drum.

Kelly claimed to have spent 20,613 hours in high places. Police and local authorities considered him a nuisance because huge crowds would gather below to watch. Traffic also became congested as a result of curious drivers craning their heads out of their windows for a look.

Foul weather or cold seasons never deterred Kelly from breaking his own records. In a particularly cold December in 1929 he sat

Flagpole sitter Alvin "Shipwreck" Kelly lends his name and talents to advertise a local used-car dealer. Such endorsements provided Kelly with a lively income during the Depression.

for 13 days, 13 hours, and 13 minutes (13 being his favorite number) atop the Paramount Hotel in New York. He was buffeted by chilling subzero winds, as rain and sleet pelted him the entire time. He spent 49 days atop a flagpole on the Atlantic City pier in 1930. When asked how he survived for so long on those tiny perches, Kelly said the secret of his success was to take five-minute catnaps every hour and to eat regularly to keep his strength up.

It is hard to imagine how anybody could be creative under the harsh conditions of the Depression. But the decade of the 1930s was a rich source of culture and new technologies. Perhaps it was the hardship itself that encouraged invention, or the fact that so many unemployed people had large amounts of time to fill, or simply desperation. In any case, future generations have had much to draw upon from those pioneer years.

The World of Tomorrow

Throughout the Depression, cities beset by economic difficulties somehow managed to put on world's fairs. These giant expositions showcased the latest advances in science and technology, which promised a more peaceful and solvent future. Chicago's Century of Progress opened on April 29, 1933, and eventually attracted 38 million people. On the success of Chicago's fair, San Francisco followed with the Golden Gate Exposition, which celebrated two of the decade's most amazing engineering feats—the Bay and Golden Gate Bridges. But the most famous world's fair was the New York World's Fair of 1939. It suitably capped the end of the decade and also marked the end of the Depression. It was truly interactive escapism that transported 32 million visitors to a cleaner, more brightly lit future where people speedily traveled in streamlined airplanes, ships, and cars and lived in idealized communities that were serviced by all technology had to offer.

Imagining the Future

The New York World's Fair opened on April 30, 1939, to celebrate the 150th anniversary of George Washington's first inauguration. The fair lasted until 1940. Built on a 1,216-acre marshland site in Flushing Meadow, Queens, the fair was split into seven major areas: amusement, entertainment, food, communications and business systems, community interests, production and distribution, and international. The highlight of the fair was its architecture, which supposedly forecast what the city of tomorrow would look like. The most distinctive structures were the two-hundred-foot ball called the Perisphere and the seven-hundred-foot spiked Trylon. The hollow Perisphere contained a huge model of Democracity, a community of the future. The unique profiles of the Perisphere and the Trylon were pasted onto every poster and banner that hung in New York. The streamlined images also graced all the fair's souvenirs.

A simulated voyage to the moon and a cigarette-smoking robot named Elecktro were other popular displays, as was the debut of a television receiver. Futurama, a $7.5 million ride that transported visitors in armchairs through a miniature fantasy representation of America in the year 1960, was the most popular ride. The spectacular Futurama attracted 28,000 people a day. The display was made of 500,000 miniature buildings, a million little trees, and 50,000 tiny streamlined, teardropshaped automobiles that traveled over a complex elevated highway network. Norman Bel Geddes designed the display for General Motors but omitted a specific type of building: visitors immediately noticed the absence of churches in the model city.

Other exhibitors at the fair included Remington Rand, General Electric, and Eastman Kodak. Fifty-eight countries (not including Germany) also built their own buildings and attractions. Sadly, during the opening stages of World War II, many of the

The Perisphere and the Trylon rise above the 1939 New York World's Fair.

international pavilions at the fair closed one by one, as Poland, followed by other countries, fell to the Axis powers.

The New York World's Fair's utopian prediction of peace was quickly canceled by escalating hostilities in Europe. In 1938 Adolf Hitler had occupied the Sudetenland in Czechoslovakia under the pretense of repatriating people of German descent. Hitler publicly promised the world that Germany would make no further territorial claims in Europe. Six months later, however, on March 15, 1939, Hitler moved to occupy the rest of Czechoslovakia. In secret, the Soviet Union signed a treaty promising not to hinder Germany in its plans to dominate the rest of Europe. In return for assuring the Germans that they were not at risk of being attacked from behind, the Soviets were to receive half of Poland, Germany's next target. Hitler invaded Poland with massive numbers of troops the following month. Britain and France declared war on Germany in accordance with an earlier pact, and thus the Second World War began. But the two countries could not aid Poland, since

to get there, they would have had to pass through Germany. Poland fell in three weeks to Hitler's blitzkrieg (lightning attack).

Back in America a political battle was raging. Many people remembered the First World War and did not want to become entangled in another conflict. "No foreign wars" became the slogan of the isolationists, who were confident that enemy troops would not cross the Atlantic Ocean to invade the United States. When the war began, Roosevelt declared the American position to the nation and the world in a fireside chat. "This nation will remain a neutral nation, but I cannot ask that every American remain neutral in thought as well. Even a neutral has a right to take account of facts. Even a neutral cannot be asked to close his mind or close his conscience." [37]

In 1937 Roosevelt, preparing for the possibility of American involvement in the war, requested a billion-dollar budget to reinforce America's defenses. The noninterventionists in Congress fought against the bill but lost by a considerable margin. Public opinion was mixed but steadily swaying toward action.

Reports of the atrocities against innocent civilians rallied groups who led consumer boycotts against aggressor nations.

Britain and France were not well equipped for all-out war and desperately needed planes and other war matériels, but Roosevelt's hands were bound by the Neutrality Acts of 1935, 1936, and 1937, which prevented any sale or transport of munitions to warring countries, even if the proposed recipients were U.S. allies. After Hitler's invasion of Poland, Congress partly conceded to Roosevelt's request and amended the most recent neutrality act. Foreign nations could now purchase arms from the United States, but only on a cash-and-carry basis. That is, buyers had to pay in cash and transport the munitions purchased on their own merchant ships. Even with this restriction, however, there was a sudden surge of demand, which revived American industry. As factories were reopened and retooled to produce war matériel, the towering problem of unemployment, which had been the bane of two presidential administrations, came to an end. As economist John Kenneth Galbraith asserts, "World War II . . . was an almost casual and pleasant experience"[38] for those who lived through the years of deprivation.

Looking Back

The Depression was the first ongoing event in history to be recorded in detail. Famous writers from the WPA arts projects, as well as diligent interviewers whose names are unknown to the general public today, showed the resilience of the human spirit with their accounts of how Americans endured the worst misery and experienced the greatest triumph in their history. This social record left a legacy for subsequent generations by permanently impressing the memories and experiences of those who lived through the Depression. The decade profoundly influenced the way people think, live, and treat others.

Despite the widespread hardship endured by all classes of society, the 1930s are remembered for many technological and cultural innovations. Conveniences taken for granted today, such as the radio, the telephone, hot and cold running water, and electricity, became widely available less than seventy years ago. New mass production techniques brought the prices of houses, cars, and other goods within the reach of the working class. Roads and cities connected all points of the map and made the country seem to shrink.

But the biggest change during the Depression was the role of the federal government. Many economists and historians question the long-term consequences of New Deal philosophies. Its policies were generous and humane: it sought to help first and foremost the people who were hungry, homeless, and unemployed. Nevertheless, the New Deal seemed to erode the principles of hard work and individualism instilled by the pioneer spirit of the nineteenth century. No longer would the federal government simply moderate events from afar. Washington assumed a more active role in regulating the affairs of commerce, business, and the welfare of the people.

Unbridled capitalism, as it was practiced up to the end of the 1920s, ceased to exist with the advent of the New Deal. New controls were placed on business and banking to prevent another catastrophic stock crash. Though Roosevelt's policy measures did not revive industry or restore full employment, they did make conditions more tolerable in the short term for people who might have otherwise starved. In addition, the planners of the New Deal arranged to install safeguards into the system, to prevent anything like the terrible events of the 1930s from happening again.

Notes

Introduction: A National Blight

1. Quoted in Rita Van Amber, *Stories and Recipes of the Great Depression of the 1930's*. Neenah, WI: Van Amber, 1986.

Chapter 1: Uncertain Times

2. Herbert Hoover, *American Individualism: The Challenge to Liberty*. New York: Garland, 1934.
3. Quoted in Charles A. Jellison, *Tomatoes Were Cheaper: Tales from the Thirties*. New York: Syracuse University Press, 1977.
4. W. W. Waters and William C. White, *BEF: The Whole Story of the Bonus Army*. New York: John Day, 1933.
5. Quoted in William E. Leuchtenburg, *Franklin D. Roosevelt and the New Deal 1932–1940*. New York: Harper & Row, 1963.
6. Quoted in Library of Congress American Life Histories, *Manuscripts from the Federal Writers' Project 1936–1940*. Accessed at www.rs6.loc.gov/wpaintro/wpahome.html
7. Quoted in Thomas C. Cochran, *The Great Depression and World War II*. Glenview, IL: Scott, Foresman, 1968.

Chapter 2: Life in the Cities and Towns

8. Quoted in Studs Terkel, *Hard Times*. New York: Pantheon Books, 1970.
9. Quoted in Jellison, *Tomatoes Were Cheaper*.
10. Quoted in Dixon Wecters, *The Age of the Great Depression 1929–1941*. New York: Macmillan, 1948.

11. Quoted in Cheryl Lynn Greenberg, *Or Does It Explode: Black Harlem in the Great Depression*. New York: Oxford University Press, 1991.
12. Quoted in Library of Congress American Life Histories, *Manuscripts from the Federal Writers' Project 1936–1940*.
13. Quoted in Terkel, *Hard Times*.
14. Quoted in Library of Congress American Life Histories, *Manuscripts from the Federal Writers' Project 1936–1940*.
15. Quoted in Terkel, *Hard Times*.
16. Quoted in Herbert Harris, *American Labor*. New Haven, CT: Yale University Press, 1938.

Chapter 3: Life in the Country

17. Quoted in Don Congdon, *The 30's: A Time to Remember*. New York: Simon & Schuster, 1962.
18. Quoted in Library of Congress American Life Histories, *Manuscripts from the Federal Writers' Project 1936–1940*.
19. Quoted in National Committee for the Defense of Political Prisoners, *Harlan Miners Speak: Report on Terrorism in the Kentucky Coal Fields*. New York: Da Capo Press, 1970.
20. Quoted in Irving Bernstein, *The Lean Years*. Boston: Houghton Mifflin, 1960.

Chapter 4: Dropping Out of Society

21. Quoted in John F. Bauman and Thomas H. Coode, *In the Eye of the Great Depression: New Deal Reporters and the Agony of the American People*. DeKalb: Northern Illinois University Press, 1988.
22. Quoted in Terkel, *Hard Times*.

23. Quoted in Thomas Minehan, *Boy and Girl Tramps of America*. New York: Grosset & Dunlap, 1934.

24. Bertha Thompson and Dr. Ben L. Reitman, *Sister of the Road*. New York: Macaulay, 1937.

25. Quoted in Nels Anderson, *The Hobo: The Sociology of the Homeless Man*. Chicago: University of Chicago Press, 1923.

26. Woody Guthrie, "Hard Travelin'," *Columbia River Collection*, Rounder 1036.

27. Quoted in Library of Congress American Life Histories, *Manuscripts from the Federal Writers' Project 1936–1940*.

28. Roger A. Bruns, *Knights of the Road: A Hobo History*. New York: Methuen Books, 1980.

Chapter 5: Crime in America

29. Quoted in Thomas M. Coffey, *The Long Thirst: Prohibition in America*. New York: Norton, 1975.

30. Stanley Walker, *The Night Club Era*. New York: Blue Ribbon Books, 1933.

31. Quoted in Richard Gid Powers, *G-Men: Hoover's FBI in American Popular Culture*. Carbondale: Southern Illinois University Press, 1983.

32. Quoted in Powers, *G-Men*.

33. Quoted in Powers, *G-Men*.

Chapter 6: Escaping the Great Depression

34. Quoted in the Editors of Time-Life Books, *This Fabulous Century: Sixty Years of American Life*. New York: Time-Life Books, 1969.

35. Quoted in Terkel, *Hard Times*.

36. June Havoc, *Early Havoc*. New York: Simon & Schuster, 1959.

Epilogue: The World of Tomorrow

37. Quoted in Fon Wyman Boardman, *The 30's: America and the Great Depression*. New York: Random House, 1967.

38. John Kenneth Galbraith, *American Capitalism: The Concept of Countervailing Power*. Boston: Houghton Mifflin, 1956.

For Further Reading

Frederick Lewis Allen, *Since Yesterday*. New York: Bantam Books, 1940. A sociological history of the people and events that shaped the 1930s.

Roger A. Bruns, *Knights of the Road: A Hobo History*. New York: Methuen Books, 1980. An in-depth look at the life and practices of the hobo in America from the earliest days of the railroad.

Jacqueline Farrell, *The Great Depression*. San Diego: Lucent Books, 1996. A general history of the Great Depression.

Jerry Stanley, *Children of the Dustbowl: The True Story of the School at Weedpatch Camp*. New York: Crown Books, 1993. A story of displaced Panhandle farmers and their children who, with the help of local school superintendent Leo Hart, helped build a school in California.

John Steinbeck, *The Grapes of Wrath*. 1939. Reprint, New York: Knopf, 1993. The seminal depression novel of the fictional Joad family and their difficult migration from drought-stricken Oklahoma to California.

Additional Works Consulted

Nels Anderson, *The Hobo: The Sociology of the Homeless Man*. Chicago: University of Chicago Press, 1923.

Isaac Asimov, *Isaac Asimov Presents From Harding to Hiroshima: An Anecdotal History of the United States from 1923–1945*. Ed. Barrington Boardman. New York: Dembner Books, 1988.

John F. Bauman and Thomas H. Coode, *In the Eye of the Great Depression: New Deal Reporters and the Agony of the American People*. DeKalb: Northern Illinois University Press, 1988.

John Baxter, *Hollywood in the Thirties*. New York: A.S. Barnes, 1968.

Robert Bendiner, *Just Around the Corner: A Highly Selective History of the Thirties*. New York: Harper & Row, 1967.

Irving Bernstein, *The Lean Years*. Boston: Houghton Mifflin, 1960.

Fon Wyman Boardman, *The 30's: America and the Great Depression*. New York: Random House, 1967.

Paul Bonnifield, *The Dust Bowl: Men, Dirt, and Depression*. Albuquerque: University of New Mexico Press, 1979.

Thomas C. Cochran, *The Great Depression and World War II*. Glenview, IL: Scott, Foresman, 1968.

Thomas M. Coffey, *The Long Thirst: Prohibition in America*. New York: Norton, 1975.

Don Congdon, *The 30's: A Time to Remember*. New York: Simon & Schuster, 1962.

Thomas H. Coode and John F. Bauman, *People, Poverty and Politics: Pennsylvanians During the Great Depression*. Lewisburg, PA: Bucknell University Press, 1981.

Joan M. Crouse, *The Homeless Transient in the Great Depression: New York State 1929–1941*. New York: State University of New York Press, 1986.

Kenneth S. Davis, *FDR: The New Deal Years 1933–1937*. New York: Random House, 1986.

Foster Rhea Dulles and Melvyn Dubofsky, *Labor in America: A History*. Arlington Heights, IL: Harlan Day, 1984.

Editors of Time-Life Books, *This Fabulous Century: Sixty Years of American Life*. New York: Time-Life Books, 1969.

Glen H. Elder Jr., *Children of the Great Depression*. Chicago: University of Chicago Press, 1974.

John Kenneth Galbraith, *American Capitalism: The Concept of Countervailing Power*. Boston: Houghton Mifflin, 1956.

Harvey Green, *The Uncertainty of Everyday Life*. New York: HarperCollins, 1992.

Cheryl Lynn Greenberg, *Or Does It Explode: Black Harlem in the Great Depression*. New York: Oxford University Press, 1991.

James N. Gregor, *American Exodus: The Dust Bowl Migration and Okie Culture in California*. New York: Oxford University Press, 1989.

Donald H. Grubbs, *Cry from the Cotton: The Southern Tenant Farmers' Union and the New Deal*. Chapel Hill: University of North Carolina Press, 1971.

Herbert Harris, *American Labor*. New Haven, CT: Yale University Press, 1938.

June Havoc, *Early Havoc*. New York: Simon & Schuster, 1959.

Herbert Hoover, *American Individualism: The Challenge to Liberty*. New York: Garland, 1934.

Charles A. Jellison, *Tomatoes Were Cheaper: Tales from the Thirties*. New York: Syracuse University Press, 1977.

David Levering Lewis, *When Harlem Was in Vogue*. New York: Knopf, 1981.

William E. Leuchtenburg, *Franklin D. Roosevelt and the New Deal 1932–1940*. New York: Harper & Row, 1963.

Library of Congress American Life Histories, *Manuscripts from the Federal Writers' Project 1936–1940*. www.rs6.loc.gov/wpaintro/wpahome.html

John H. Lyle, *The Dry and Lawless Years*. Englewood Cliffs, NJ: Prentice-Hall, 1960.

Robert S. McElvaine, *Down & Out in the Great Depression: Letters from the "Forgotten Man."* Chapel Hill: University of North Carolina Press, 1983.

John Mebane, *Collecting Nostalgia: The First Guide to the Antiques of the 30's and 40's*. New Rochelle, NY: Arlington House, 1972.

Thomas Minehan, *Boy and Girl Tramps of America*. New York: Grosset & Dunlap, 1934.

Felix Morely, ed., *Aspects of the Depression*. Chicago: University of Chicago Press, 1968.

George E. Mowry and Blaine A. Brownell, *The Urban Nation 1920–1980*. New York: Hill & Wang, 1965.

National Committee for the Defense of Political Prisoners, *Harlan Miners Speak: Report on Terrorism in the Kentucky Coal Fields*. New York: Da Capo Press, 1970.

Judith O'Sullivan, *The Great American Comic Strip: One Hundred Years of Cartoon Art*. Boston: Little, Brown, 1990.

Cabell Phillips, *The New York Times Chronicle of American Life: From the Crash to the Blitz 1929–1939*. New York: Macmillan, 1969.

Richard Gid Powers, *G-Men: Hoover's FBI in American Popular Culture*. Carbondale: Southern Illinois University Press, 1983.

Edgar Eugene Robinson and Vaughn Davis Bornet, *Herbert Hoover: President of the United States*. Stanford, CA: Hoover Institution Press, 1975.

Elliot A. Rosen, *Hoover, Roosevelt, and the Brains Trust: From Depression to New Deal*. New York: Columbia University Press, 1977.

Peter Schwed, *God Bless Pawnbrokers*. New York: Dodd, Mead, 1975.

Jacqueline Gorden Sherman, *The Oklahomans in California During the Depression Decade 1931–1941*. Berkeley and Los Angeles: University of California Press, 1970.

David W. Stowe, *Swing Changes: Big Band Jazz in New Deal America*. Cambridge, MA: Harvard University Press, 1994.

Studs Terkel, *Hard Times*. New York: Pantheon Books, 1970.

Bertha Thompson and Dr. Ben L. Reitman, *Sister of the Road*. New York: Macaulay, 1937.

Rita Van Amber, *Stories and Recipes of the Great Depression of the 1930's*. Neenah, WI: Van Amber Publishers, 1986.

Leo Walker, *The Wonderful Era of the Great Dance Bands*. New York: Da Capo Press, 1990.

Stanley Walker, *The Nightclub Era*. New York: Blue Ribbon Books, 1933.

W. W. Waters and William C. White, *BEF: The Whole Story of the Bonus Army*. New York: John Day, 1933.

T.H. Watkind, *The Great Depression: America in the 1930's*. Boston: Little, Brown, 1993.

Dixon Wecters, *The Age of the Great Depression 1929–1941*. New York: Macmillan, 1948.

David Manning White and Robert H. Abel, eds., *The Funnies: An American Idiom*. London: Collier-Macmillan, 1963.

Index

Picture Credits

Cover photo: Library of Congress

AP/Wide World Photos, 10, 43, 53, 62, 68, 73, 77, 84

Archive Photos, 26, 61

Brown Brothers, 13 (top), 15, 24, 54, 57, 59, 60, 64, 67, 75, 78, 81, 82

The Depression Years As Photographed by Arthur Rothstein, Dover Publications, Inc., 29, 38, 44, 49

Library of Congress, 9, 11, 13 (bottom), 16, 17, 18, 20, 21 (both), 25, 31, 32, 41, 45, 47, 65, 72

National Archives, 76

Sonya Noskowiak, courtesy Arthur F. Noskowiak, The John Steinbeck Collection, Stanford University Libraries, 42

Stock Montage, Inc., 28, 69

About the Author

Dennis Nishi is a freelance writer and graphic designer. He has a degree in English from Long Beach State University in California. His work has been published in several small magazines and newspapers, including the *Long Beach Press Telegram*. This is his first book for Lucent.